ROSELLA VANTAGGI

S IENA

sub rbs and province

EVER Y USEFUL INFORMATION FOR THE TOURIST

192 pages with 135
coloured plates
Street and monumental-plan
of the Town

Esclusivista per la vendita
ROMBONI MARIO
Via C. Battisti 20 - Tel. 283263
SIENA

GENERAL INDEX

Index

4

List of the most well known artists mentioned in this guide-book:

P = Painter   **S** = Sculptor   **A** = Architect

Agnolo di Ventura **S A** Siena 1325-1348
Andrea del Sarto **P** Firenze 1486-1530
Antonio da Sangallo il Giovane **S A** Firenze 1483-1546
Antonio da Sangallo il Vecchio **S A** Firenze 1453-1534
Arnolfo di Cambio Colle V. Elsa **A S** 1245-1302
Barili Antonio **A Int.** Siena 1453-1516
Bartolo di Fredi **P** Siena 1330-1410
Beccafumi Domenico **P S** Cast. Berard. (Siena) 1486-1551
Benedetto da Maiano **A S** Firenze 1442-1497
Bernini Gian Lorenzo **A P S** Napoli 1598-1680
Botticelli Sandro **P** Firenze 1445-1510
Buontalenti Bernardo **A P S** Firenze 1536-1608
Canova Antonio **P S** Treviso 1757-1822
Casolani Alessandro **P** Siena 1552-1606
Casolani Cristoforo **P** Siena ?-1630
Conca Sebastiano **P** Gaeta 1680-1764
Coppo di Marcovaldo **P** Firenze 1225-1274
Cozzarelli Giacomo **A S** Siena 1453-1515
Cozzarelli Guidoccio **P** Siena 1450-1516/17
Domenico di Bartolo **P** Asciano (Siena) 1440-1445
Domenico di Niccolò dei Cori **Int.** Siena 1362-1453
Donatello (Donato dei Bardi) **S** Firenze 1386-1466·
Duccio di Buoninsegna **P** Siena 1255-1318/19
Dupré Giovanni **S.** Siena 1817-1882
Federighi Antonio **A S** Siena 1420-1490
Fei Paolo di Giovanni **P** Siena 1372-1410/11
Fra Bartolomeo della Porta **P** Firenze 1472-1517
Francesco del Tonghio **Int.** Siena 1300-1388
Francesco di Giorgio Martini **A P S** 1439-1502
Fuga Ferdinando **A** Firenze 1699-1781
Fungai Bernardino **P** Siena 1460-1516
Gerini Lorenzo di Niccolò **P** Firenze 1400-1500 circa

Ghiberti Lorenzo **A P S** Firenze 1368-1415
Ghirlandaio Domenico **A P S** Firenze 1378-1455
Giotto **A P S** Vicchio (Firenze) 1267-1337
Giovanni di Paolo **P** Siena 1403-1482
Giovanni di Turino **S** Siena 1385-1455
Girolamo da Cremona **P** Attivo a Siena 1467-1485
Girolamo del Pacchia **P** Siena 1477-1533
Giuliano da Maiano **A Int.** Firenze 1432-1490
Giunta Pisano **P** Pisa 1229-1245
Goro di Neroccio **S** Siena 1387-1456
Guido da Siena **P** attivo sec. XIII
Guido del Tonghia **S** attivo Siena 1395
Jacopo della Quercia **S** Siena 1371-1438
Lapo di Pietro **A S** Siena ?-1340
Lippi Filippino **P** Prato 1457-1504
Lorenzetti Ambrogio **P** Siena 1319-1347
Marrina Lorenzo **S** Siena 1476-1534
Martini Simone **P** Siena 1285-1344
Masaccio **P** S. Giov. Valdarno 1401-1428
Matteo di Giovanni **P** Sansepolcro 1430-1495
Memmi Lippo **P** Siena 1317-1347
Michelozzi Michelozzo **A S** Firenze 1396-1472
Neroccio di Bartolomeo Landi **A S** Firenze 1447-1500
Nicola Pisano **S** (pugliese-toscano?) 1220-1278/87
Paolo di Martino **A Inc.** attivo Siena 1376-1426
Partini Giuseppe **A** Siena 1842-1895
Perugino (Vannucci Pietro detto il) **P** Perugia 1450-1523
Peruzzi Baldassare **A P** Siena 1481-1536
Piero della Francesca **P** Sansepolcro 1420-1492
Pinturicchio **P** Perugia 1454-1513
Pisano Giovanni **A S** Pisa? 1245/50-1314
Pollaiolo Pietro **P S** Firenze 1443-1496
Pontormo Jacopo **P** Empoli 1494-1556
Riccio (Bartolomeo Neroni d.) **P S** Siena 1500-1571/73
Robbia Ambrogio (della) **A S ceram.** Firenze 1470-1527
Robbia Andrea (della) **S ceram.** Firenze 1435-1525
Robbia Luca (della) **S ceram.** Firenze 1399-1482
Rossellino Antonio **S** Firenze 1427-1479
Rossellino Bernardo **A S** Firenze 1409-1464
Salimbeni Ventura **P** Siena 1567-1613
Sano di Matteo **A S** Siena 1392-1434
Sano di Pietro **P Min.** Siena 1406-1481
Sassetta (Stefano di Giovanni d.) **P** Siena-Arezzo? 1392-1451
Scalza Ippolito **A S** Orvieto 1532-1617
Segna di Bonaventura **P** Siena 1298-1331
Signorelli Luca **P** Cortona 1441-1523
Sodoma (Giov. Antonio Bazzi d.) **P** Vercelli 1447-1549
Spinello Aretino **P** Arezzo 1373-1410
Taddeo di Bartolo **P** Siena 1362-1422
Tegliacci Niccolò (di Ser Sozzo) **P** Siena ?-1363
Tino di Camaino **S** Siena 1285-1337
Turino di Sano **S** Siena 1382-1427
Ugolino di Nerio **P** Siena attivo sec. XIV
Vanni Andrea **P** Siena 1330-1414
Vanni Francesco **P Inc.** Siena 1563-1610
Vasari Giorgio **A P** Arezzo 1511-1574
Vecchietta (Lorenzo di Pietro d.) **A P S** Siena 1412-1480
Vignola (Jacopo Barozzi d.) Vignola (Modena) 1507-1573
Zuccari Federico **A P** Pesaro-Urbino 1540-1609

THE ART AND HISTORY OF SIENA

« SIENA OPENS HER HEART OUT TO YOU MUCH WIDER THAN THIS DOOR! ». These words are written on the front of Porta Camollia (COR MAGIS TIBI SENA PANDIT), which is the Northernmost and also most important of the Sienese gates. This well-wishing Sienese embrace, which greeted foreigners to the city a long time ago, still welcomes tourists of today, all going to show the hospitable nature of Siena and the Sienese.

Siena and the Sienese: in very few parts of the world will one find a truer and more authentic union; a city made to measure for its people who, in turn, jealously watch over their own city, proudly and wisely maintaining its institutions and monuments as well as preserving the memory of its past.

As a matter of fact, although the city has been through many stormy events – namely sieges, civil struggles and political disturbances – seen each and every kind of disaster and witnessed the highest heroic acts, in spite of all this it has managed to preserve intact its original appearance of a medieval city, its own history and monuments. And it is this particular air of bygone times that gives Siena its deep charm.

To the tourist arriving here either by the ancient road of Francigena or Romea, or else via the modern-day route from Florence, Siena appears in a gradual shading of brick-red buildings with their roof-tiles in ascending layers, the city branches and spreads out over the hills, with elongated houses, slim church steeples that suddenly go uphill and downdale; all in a lively and uneven landscape that is dominated by the contours of the monumental buildings.

Situated on the heights and practically in the centre of southern Tuscany, the city of Siena rises up on the ridge of three hills that extend from Croce del Travaglio, the topographic centre of the built up area. Also branching out from here are the three ridgeways which go to make up the city's road network, namely Via di Città, Banchi di Sopra and Banchi di Sotto. These roads continue along the ridge leading into other roads until they arrive at the most important gates (or Porta) of the last of the city walls to be constructed and which still stands to this very day.

They are Porta San Marco which leads to Grosseto, Porta Camollia which leads to Florence and Porta Romana which, as the name suggests, leads to Rome. The actual nucleus of the city is, therefore, modelled according to the lay out of these three hills that are separated by as many steep and almost impregnable valleys, large parts of which are today still in their natural state or else cultivated into gardens and orchards.

It follows that from the very beginning the city's perimeter assumed a winding and characteristic appearance roughly in the shape of a star and which remained unchanged in spite of the city's further development. The clayey nature of the soil is linked to another of the city's characteristics, that is the presence of a number of springs which, in the past, greatly influenced Siena's actual existence: hence the need to strengthen them. The Sienese, in fact, right from very ancient times, tried their hardest to exploit even the smallest trickle from the subterranean layer of clay, channelling the water into the numerous public fountains and private wells, via a long network of criss-crossing underground tunnels. Among the public fountains, the most famous ones are Fonte di Follonica, Fonte d'Ovile, Fonte Nuova, Fonte Gaia and, most of all, Fonte Branda, the oldest and most abundant in water, situated at the foot of a cliff.

At the edge of this cliff stands the church of St. Dominick which in the past aided the development of industries and contributed towards making the inhabitants of the neighbourhood wealthy. At first glance, the whole of Siena seems to be enclosed within the mighty circle of its medieval walls, clinging to its hills, with its buildings terraced on the slopes. Very few towns present such sharp differences in their ground levels and offer such varied and interesting panoramic views. From the windows of the houses, the steep streets and the roads skirting the edges of the valleys, the view dominates the surrounding undulating countryside and sweeps the distant horizon, especially to the South and Southeast, where the landscape is wide and spacious. Right up to Mount Amiata and the heights in front of the lakes of Chiusi, Montepulciano and Valdichiana.

On entering the city, one notices straightaway that

the roads paved with cobblestones are without pavements. The buildings are tall and lined one up against another, often not allowing even the side roads to separate them. In fact, when passing underneath the houses, one will find arches linking parallel roads, some suggestive courtyards and dark, closed-in entrance halls, intricate lanes and narrow, small squares. All these aspects give Siena its very fascinating appearance and, together, forms its history without which nobody could ever understand this very characteristic city, this corner of the Middle Ages that has succeeded in reaching us, which does not exist exclusively for its splendid monuments and for its numerous works of art, save that alongside this miracle of art stands the city itself: a city of distant even though uncertain and legendary origins. Some say that Siena was founded by the Gauls, others instead sustain that its founder was Senio the son of Remus, from which the Roman she-wolf has been adopted as emblem of the city. The hypothesis of it once being an Etruscan centre is very uncertain, because the archeological findings of the 18th and 19th centuries discovered in certain hypogea (underground chambers) of the city belong to a period late enough to make the first existence of an inhabited centre coincide with the period of the Roman Republic. However, there is more certain information regarding the Roman colony founded either by the Triumvinians or, perhaps by Augustus in 29 B.C. and called by the following names: Sainy by the geographer Ptolemy, Sena Julia by the Peutingerian Table, « Colonia Senensis » by Plinius the Elder, Sena Etruriae to distinguish it from Sena Gallica (today called Senigallia).

Recently the hypothesis was brought forward that this colony might have actually stood at the foot of Montagnola Senese, between Brema, Spannocchia and Stigliano, in the locality of Old Siena, and that during the encroaching Barbarian invasion, the inhabitants took refuge on the highest of the hills, where Siena stands today, and erected Castel Vecchia which is the oldest nucleus of the present-day city. Siena's conversion to Christianity can be traced to the end of the 4th century and, perhaps, the following century saw the institution of the « Vescovado », Bishop's residence, which disappeared together with the colony, during the first Barbarian invasions and which the Arezzo records, when referring to the secular fighting between the two cities as to the diocesan boundaries, show as being restored at the time of King Rotari and the Sienese Bishop Mauro.

Very little is known about the period relating to the fall of the Roman Empire and the early Middle Ages. However, what is certain is that Siena, hindered in its territorial expansion by the greater power of Florence, situated far away from the sea and open only towards the difficult Maremma country, experienced sieges and devastations, internal struggles and terrible plagues. Governed by the Gastaldis under the Longobards, then by the Contis under the Carolingians, Siena passed into the hands of the Bishops towards the middle of the 11th century. The latter managed to exert a vast temporal power forcing into submission even some important feudatories. In the mid-12th century, also the Bishops were ousted from power by the Consuls, who substituted the clerical government with a lay one.

And it was in this period that Siena came to know its highest political fame and greatest territorial expansion, due mostly for reasons of an economic nature. After having obtained substantial privileges, first from Emperor Henry VI and then Emperor Otto IV, in exchange for its Ghibelline support, Siena saw an increase in its own trade. The Sienese merchants had business deals in many European countries and they began preparing themselves in becoming the bankers of the Pope. Such prosperity, however, provoked fierce fighting between the feudatories and the nearby cities and, most of all with the other great Tuscan city, namely Guelf Florence. In fact, Siena which introduced itself as being the centre of the Tuscan Ghibellines and welcomed exiled Florentines, became its direct rival.

The very first fights between them broke out in 1141, and in 1235 Florence managed to impose on Siena a very hard peace treaty which, among other things, deprived it of Poggibonsi and Montalcino. However, once again, the peace brought with it much development in Siena's trade and art. In 1236, there was an uprising against the governing of noble families and a Council was established comprising of 24 citizens, out of which 12 nobles and 12 townfolk, who were handed the administration of the city.

During this 24-man government, which was later called

Servants of the People and Commune, a decidedly Ghibelline policy was followed together with greater trust in Emperor Frederick II, so much so that in 1251, Siena allied with Pisa, Pistoia and the Ghibellines of Arezzo against Florence and the Tuscan Guelf party. After an initial phase in favour of Florence, the war was re-kindled in Maremma and in Valdichiana and fighting alongside the Sienese were the exiled Florentine Ghibellines and the contingents sent by Manfredi. Siena came out of the war with two great victories, the first in May 1260 under the city walls and the other at Montaperti in Val d'Arbia on the 4th September, 1260. Dante's words « Great havoc that made the river Arbia run red », vividly recall the event.

The victory at Montaperti resulted in Siena's political and military supremacy over Tuscany and also a noticeable economic leadership. In this way, Siena became the transit point of all the trade that crossed Italy: a valuable currency was adopted for exchange purposes namely the silver gross, large banking firms were set up which operated all over Italy, and profitable trade links with the East were established. The city was, therefore, rich and free and these propitious circumstances enabled the arts and studies to thrive and develop. The Sienese University was founded which was a real State university; renowned most of all for the value attributed to its faculties of Law and Medicine. It also produced a flourishing number of orators, men of letters and poets, such as Ciampolo Ugurgieri, translator of Virgil and translator into the vernacular of Aesop, Cecco Angiolieri – Dante's eccentric friend, Benuccio Salimbeni, Folcacchiero Folcacchieri, Folgore of San Gimignano who was chorister of the Spendereccia Brigade and Nuccio di Piacente, maternal ancestor of St. Catherine. This same period saw the founding of the Santa Maria della Scala Hospital, the Society of Flagellants, the Misericordia Society, as well as the construction of the basilicas of St. Francis and St. Dominick together with the institution of numerous other brotherhoods and religious societies.

However, the triumph of Ghibellinism in Tuscany dealt a hard blow to Siena, where in the meantime the Consuls had been substituted by a « Podestà » flanked by the Leader of the People. The ex-communication inflicted by the Pope on the Ghibelline city together with other economic and political factors, such as the death of King Manfredi who sided with Siena in the battle of Montaperti, soon caused an upheaval in the city. The rich Sienese merchants passed over to Guelfism in order to ensure for themselves easier profits, while within the city the contention between the nobles and townsfolk worsened. On the 11th June, 1269, the Sienese ere defeated on the plain lying between Colle Val d'Elsa and Monteriggioni. This was followed by the establishment of a Council made up of 36 representatives of all the parties, later to be substituted by one comprising 15 members (1280) and later still, by a nine-member government which remained in power until 1355 supporting a Guelf policy and maintaining friendly relations with Florence.

This nine-member government comprised of popular and merchant families but constituted an oligarchy of important merchants and bankers, and proved undoubtedly, after the consular one, to be the best government that the Sienese had ever had. It assured the continued prosperity of the dominion, embellished the city with illustrious monuments, such as Palazzo Pubblico, the Cathedral and the most beautiful buildings adorning the city, erected the actual city walls and marked the most flourishing period for the University.

But the continuous battles, the famine of 1326 and the terrible plague of 1348 caused widespread discontent among the people and provoked an uprising that brought about the fall of the nine-member government. There followed a variety of short-lived governments, until the year 1399 when Siena gave in to Gian Galeazzo Visconti, Duke of Milan. But in 1404, Visconti died and the Sienese regained their freedom; a freedom embittered by the continuous domestic and foreign stugglees, even though St. Catherine and St. Bernardine made overwhelming and persuasive preachings in those years about keeping the peace. After a government of ten Priors and Nobles, in 1482 Pandolfo Petrucci took over Siena and held power right until 1512. However Siena was by that time at the mercy of much greater powers: in October 1530 the troops of Charles V, King of Spain, entered the city.

Soon a revolt broke out and in July 1552, the Spaniards retreated after three days of bitter fighting. However, two years later, an army of Germans, Spaniards and Italians led by Gian Giacomo de' Medici laid siege to Siena. It was a hard and terrible siege which the Sienese tried their hardest to resist and, as a last resort they decided to rid their city of all those persons who were considered useless. But every act of heroism proved in vain and on the 17th April, 1555, Siena was forced to surrender. In 1559, following the Cateau-Cambresis Treaty, the city together with its entire State finally fell under Cosimo I.

After the Medici, Siena together with the rest of Tuscany, passed over to the house of Lorraine; then at the time of Napoleon, it acted as chief town of the Department of the River Ombrone before returning to Lorraine. It participated in the Risorgimento and in 1859 it was the first Tuscan city to concede its annexation to the Kingdom of Italy.

Siena's history is, therefore, one of wars, of stormy, dark events, of troubled episodes, of great splendour and of supreme heroism. In spite of all this, the city underwent an exceptionally rich artistic development, so much so that during the late 13th and early 14th centuries, it became one of the major protagonists of the Italian as well as European artistic civilisations. And yet, Siena was neither rich nor lucky; in fact it is situated in a region which although being very picturesque, lacks in natural resources, is far from the sea and as the city was forced to expand, its only outlet was towards the poor and wild land of Maremma, in order to protect the State and its trade. Also the rich Sienese families who true to the proverb « Quick to spend but just as quick to earn », really contributed very little to the expansion of the city's art works, with the exception, of course, of their rich patrician villas. Also during the period in which the famous creative personalities began establishing themselves, these rich families were already in rapid decline. As for the people and the governments that more or less represented them, both lived on for centuries amidst the rumble of warfare and were almost always divided by the contrasting factions. The fact of not being favoured with riches nor with power and national wealth made Siena interpret the steady boom in the arts and all the spiritual activities in general as being a typically popular and universal phenomenon that finds its initial and most profound reasons in the nature, tendencies and actual character of its citizens and in the inspirations and ideals of the various institutions that governed its existence. Splendidly ambitious and superb, and at the same time full of mystic impetus, elegant and worldly yet capable of reaching into the deepest and most fragile recesses of spirituality, fantastically fairy-like but realist to the point of a newscast or document. Art was for Siena a true mirror of an extremely compound and variegated society, but exceptionally up-to-date in its tastes and customs even in the poor classes; a society whose groups and members right from the State Bench to the Guilds of craftsmen, from the great monastic communities to the popular brother-hoods, all consider art as an indispensable attribute to their dignity, or rather, their actual existence. And even if the beginnings of such a dazzling and prolong-ed art tradition were modest and tardy in coming, in the space of a few centuries Siena acquired its rich, artistic patrimony, for which it is so rightly renowned. The 12th century saw the construction of many beau-tiful buildings, numerous towers and nobles' residen-ces, churches of modest dimensions though pure romanesque in their architecture, namely San Pietro alla Magione, San Donato, San Cristofaro, San Marco and San Quirico. Others unfortunately have either been destoyed or incorporated in successive cons-tructions. The buildings changed all of a sudden from these minor works to the truly great national enter-prise of the Cathedral, which summarises in the complex story of its construction, the Sienese archi-tectural leanings from the fall of Romanesque to the birth of Gothic. The flourishing Gothic architecture can be witnessed in many splendid Sienese buildings, take for example the upper part of the Cathedral's facade, the apse which was much later enlarged, and the vaults above the main nave.

The Gothic period saw the construction of the Baptistry facade and the huge churches of the Mendicant Orders, such as St. Francis, St. Dominick and St. Mary of the Servants, wherein the spacious interiors seem to diminish and vanish in the shadows of the tall exposed beams and fit in with the vast expanses of the side walls with their high ogival windows. In the two centuries during which the Cathedral was built, Siena acquired its most characteristic features and developed its own unmistakable style even in civil architecture. The most accomplished work and highest expression of this style is Palazzo Pubblico, which later inspired the design of the other city buildings such as Palazzo Sansedoni, Chigi-Saraceni, Palazzo del Capitano and even Palazzo Marsili and Palazzo Buonsignori that were constructed in the mid-15th century.

Originating from this style and representing a typical motif of the local architecture is the « Sienese arch », which is a combination of two elements of Pisan origin, the barrier-type arch and the Muslim-type deep sickle arch. Sienese architecture displays its originality even in the fountains and gates: the aforementioned Fonte d'Ovile, Fonte di Follonica and the famous Fontebranda, as well as Porta Romana, Porta Pispini and Porta d'Ovile, which were built not only for defence purposes, but also to give a grand stateliness to the main gateways to the city.

In the early 15th century, Siena too welcomed the novelties of the Renaissance period, with the works of the two Florentines, Bernardo Rossellini and Giuliano da Maiano, and the Sienese Antonio Federighi (1420-1490), Francesco di Giorgio Martini (1439-1502) and Baldassare Peruzzi (1481-1536).

During the Baroque period, the architects working in Siena were Damiano Schifandini, Flaminio del Turco, Giovanni Fontana and Benedetto Giovanelli, who are all attributed with numerous buildings of a harmonious and well-proportioned style.

In the field of sculpture, Siena did not have any particular school until the arrival of Nicola and Giovanni Pisano, the former sculptured the magnificent pulpit of the Cathedral and the latter the statues of the facade, and they both had numerous and very valid followers.

Sienese sculpture later reached supreme heights with Jacopo della Quercia whose creations include Fonte Gaia and certain parts of Fonte Battesimale, which incidentally Ghiberti and Donatello also worked on.

Siena reached the highest acclaims in art mainly with its paintings. After Guido da Siena's Madonna, one of the first great Sienese paintings, comes Duccio di Buoninsegna, who is considered the founder of the Sienese school and who found the Gothic style ideally suited to his own spirit. Then come Simone Martini and the Lorenzetti's who bequeathed Siena their greatest works and who also had a faithful band of followers amongst whom stand out for their personality and style, Barna, Taddeo di Bartolo, Jacopo di Mino del Pellicciaio and Paolo di Giovanni Fei.

Also the successive centuries brought some famous names to Sienese painting, names such as Sassetta, Giovanni di Paolo, Vecchietta, Matteo di Giovanni, Francesco di Giorgio Martini in the 15th century and Sodoma, Domenico Beccafumi and Baldassare Meruzzi in the 16th century.

With the coming of Mannerism, the Sienese school suffered a decline and was left without any masters of great importance. But it should be pointed out that the Sienese also achieved great perfection in the minor arts. Goldsmiths, inlayers, miniaturists, all excelled in those works where the artisan technique was combined with their elegant sense of decoration and the most authentic expression of their creative talent.

More than a medieval city Siena is a city of art.

And to get better acquainted and learn to love and appreciate Siena, we suggest a walk through its tiny alleys and in between the old houses, where every corner and stone holds a bit of history. Let us enter the museums and churches that sparkle with priceless masterpieces, astounding works, almost as if in a competition where all the great artists and sculptors display a shining example of their immortal art.

But Siena is also the Palio, which is a demonstration well-exceeding the proportions of a normal folkloristic display or revival of some historic event. The Palio is a feast of the people, a sort of ritual, during which the city reveals its true colours, collects together all its personal likes and dislikes and relives with enthusiasm and nostalgic passion that fantastic dream of its past grandeur.

On the days when the Palio is run, the air is live with atmosphere and even on the days previous, the seventeen districts bustle with activity and fervour. The city of yesterday continues to live alongside the city of today, in a beautiful framework rising out of the historic and artistic surroundings that are unique in the world.

Via di Città - Loggia of the Merchants - Piazza del Campo - The Gaia Fountain - The Palazzo Pubblico - Chapel of the Square - The Mangia Tower - The Civic Museum - Palazzo Piccolomini: the States Archives.

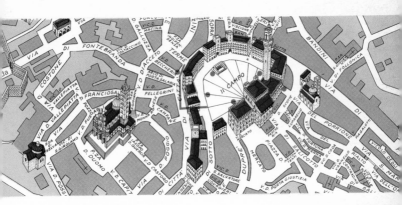

At the beginning of VIA DI CITTÀ, at number 2, lies **Loggia della Mercanzia**, also known as Loggia of the Merchants or of St. Paul, and once the ancient site of the Tribunal of Shopkeepers. It is an elegant and solid build-ing, whose architecture is a splendid example of the period marking the passage from Gothic to Renaissance. It was designed by Sano di Matteo (1417-1428) and built by Pietro del Pinella (1428-1444), and comprises three arches over the facade and an arch over each lower side, all in the Renaissance style, whilst the niches and statues adorning the pillars overlooking Via di Città are decidedly Gothic. The statues date from the late 15th century, the two side ones – St. Paul on the right and St. Peter on the left – are by Vecchietta (1458-1460), and the two in the middle – St. Victor and St. Ansano – are by Antonio Federighi (1456-1463). After the brilliant genius of Jacopo della Quercia come these two great Sienese sculptors of the 15th century. The beautiful wrought-iron gate railings date from 1887 and were designed by Augusto Corbi.

Out of the two marble counters, which in the interior close off the colonnade at its two shorter sides, the most renowned is that on the right by Federighi (1464), bearing the figures of five characters from Roman history. The other counter with the four Cardinal Virtues is the work of Urbano da Cortona.

The upper floor, which was added in 1600, is the Seat of the Society of the United, founded in 1657. and the Provincial Tourist Authority. On the left of the Loggia, forming an angle between Banchi di Sopra and Vicolo di San Pietro, is an ancient tower house, flanked by a 14th century building with a three-mullioned window.

From VIA DI CITTA', which runs almost along the edge of the highest hill and hides among the most ancient buildings, one can discover with each step the tangled mass of this truly tentacular city that winds along the buttresses of the hills offering panoramic views of the horizon, then carry on into VICOLO SAN PIETRO and descend into PIAZZA DEL CAMPO or simply CAMPO.

PIAZZA DEL CAMPO

All that there is to write has already been written about this square; it is illustrated in all the postcards, documentaries, prints and books the whole world over. And yet, when we look into this spacious shell, with its resounding walls, its beauty all poetry and spectacle like an enormous stage where we are the actors, we are overcome with an intense emotion.

Uniting here, where Siena's entire history has occurred, are three hills on which the city stands. The altimetrical differences in the ground level, in fact, seems to have inspired its original shell shape. Confronting us is one of those phenomena wherein the conditions and difficulties caused by nature diminish and, instead, are transformed into true works of technique and, most of all, of art. The

ground is paved at the edges, while the middle, since the year 1347, is paved with tiles placed in a herringbone pattern and subdivided by stripes of white stone into nine sectors, as a reminder of the Nine-member Government, when Palazzo Pubblico and Piazza del Campo were constructed.

Resulting from the need, in the 12th century, to channel and deviate rainwater on to the irregular and barren ground, Campo is deservedly renowned as being one of the most beautiful squares in the whole world and through its effective scenography, it takes us straightaway back to the days of those industrious Middle Ages which have given us the civilisation of free cities. Some of the most important events in Siena's city life took place right in this square, for example the dramatic battles or peace treaties between its opposing factions, and when the Sienese prayed and hoped while awaiting news of the victory at Montaperti.

It was here that Lady Ausilia brought, tied to the ribbon of her plaits, thirty-six Florentine prisoners captured at Montaperti and, also here, Provenzan Salvani, the victor of that battle, went around the streets begging from his fellow-citizens until he had collected the ten thousand gold florins needed to release his friend Vigna, held prisoner by Charles of Puglia. Pier Pettinaio and San Bernardino held great talks here just as though it was an open-air hall. Finally, in 1555, it was here that the people lived through days of terror, from the siege by Charles V to the fall of the Republic.

THE GAIA FOUNTAIN – After having admired the square in its entirety, it is time to observe its splendid monuments.

Standing almost in the centre of the semicircle, at the border of the tiled road, is the Gaia Fountain, built on the same site where once stood another fountain dating from the 14th century. It is the work of JACOPO DI PIE-TRO, otherwise known as DELLA QUERCIA, probably due to the fact that his family came from Quercegrossa, on the outskirts of Siena about (1374-Siena 1438). His art, along-side the Gothic elements ruling at that time in tradition with Sienese art, shows a clear presence once again of volumes and classical statues, anticipating the nearby Renaissance works and costituting, above all, one of the very first examples of that composure and harmony that soon was to dominate the fields of architecture, sculpture and painting.

Designed in the shape of a rectangular basin surrounded on three sides by a high parapet and built between the years 1409 and 1419, the fountain appears to us as a great exultation of snow-white marble and crystal clear water murmuring in the rose-coloured shell of Campo.

Perhaps, its name derives from this and not just from the fact that there was great rejoicing by the people at the time of its inauguration in 1414 (?).

The fountain is fed by an aqueduct dating from 1344 and measuring about twenty-five kilometres in lenght. The original sculptures that adorned the Gaia Fountain are now kept in the Palazzo Pubblico, because in 1868 they were substituted with other faithful reproductions, made by Tito Sarrocchi, for fear of them ageing and deteriorating. The bas-reliefs, situated in the niches, represent from left to right: **The Creation of Adam, Wisdom, Hope, Power, Prudence, The Madonna and Child between two Angels, Justice, Charity, Moderation, Faith, The Expelling of Adam and Eve from the Garden of Eden.**

THE PALAZZO PUBBLICO

Among this amphitheatre of famous buildings, glowing red in the sun and reaching high in the sky, the invariable and unique backdrop of the square is formed by the Palazzo Pubblico with its slender Manopia Tower and the Chapel of the square underneath. Majestic and elegant, tall, slim and picturesque in its structure and in the well-proportioned distribution of its entire area, the PALAZZO PUBBLICO is considered the most famous of all the Tuscan Gothic buildings and the most remarkable example of Sienese civil architecture that tends, more than others, to use lighter and slender architectural lines and a refined taste in pictorial decoration.

The story of its construction is strongly connected to Siena's political and economic history. Work started after the year 1250, according to documents of that period; by 1299, the entire main nucleus was completed while, in 1305, construction work began on the two wings. The building was terminated in 1310 and it maintained its original shape until the year 1680 and in the early 18th century, when additions were made and certain parts were raised. However, these latter works did not alter the style of the building's frontal aspect.

The delicate colour combination of the foundation's silver-grey travertine marble and the warm, rosy brickwork of the upper areas, together with the precious splendour of the white and black coats-of-arms which, like enamel works, stud the drapery; the oscillating play of light and

shadow of the windows, heavily stressing the design of the arches on the ground floor, as well as the light, wide expanse of the graceful three-mullioned windows on the upper floors and, also, the slender linearity of the buildings' cornices, all go to show in such an admirable way how Siena's exquisite sense of pictorial art is impressed even in its secular architecture.

Between the mullioned windows on the last floor, that is crowned with small arches and merlons, lies a huge copper disc bearing the monogram of Christ, symbol of St. Bernard, and, at the sides, stand two wolves made of stone. The Palazzo Pubblico was once the seat of the Dominion and Podesta of the ancient Sienese Republic; today it acts as the Town Hall.

THE FACADE – On the left of the Palazzo, at the bottom, stands the Chapel of the Square – CAPPELLA DI PIAZZA – which was built to fulfil a vow made by the Sienese during the plague in 1348 and, surmounting it is the Mangia Tower. In fact, the actual work on the Chapel was begun in 1352 by Domenico d'Agostino and completed around the year 1376 by Giovanni di Cecco, who saw to the final positioning of the pillars and the roof.

The pillars bear statues of saints that were sculptured between the years 1377 and 1381. Starting with the right pillar, going round it and then moving to the left pillar, we can view **St. James the Greater** by Bartolomeo di Tommè and by Mariano di Angelo; **St. John the Baptist** above and the **Younger St. James** below by Lando di Stefano; **St. Thomas** by Giovanni di Turino. Adorning the Chapel parapets are bas-reliefs which were taken from another monument dating from the 13th century and, which were partly re-done by Enea Becheroni in 1846. The wrought-iron railings are the work of Conte di Lello Orlandi and Pietruccio di Betto (14th century). Situated near the altar is a valuable fresco by Sodoma, representing the « **Madonna with Saints and the Eternal** » (1537) which, unfortunately, has suffered irreparable deterioration.

THE MANGIA TOWER – Standing completely to the left of the Palazzo Pubblico is the MANGIA TOWER, which cuts the horizon with its pure and slender lines and which is marvellous proof not only of the architectonic genius but also of the valid engineering sense possessed by the skilled workmen of that era. The Tower's name is derived from Giovanni di Duccio, known as « Mangiaguadagni » (meaning profit eater) or simply « Mangia » (eater), who was one of the first assigned by the Commune with the task of ringing the bells. Even the mechanical device that was installed to chime the hour and, which existed right until 1780, was nicknamed « The Mangia ».

The brick chimney was built by the two brothers Minuccio

and Francesco di Rinaldo from Perugia (1338-1348). After the thin cornice rises up the first crowning in travertine marble bearing the two coats-of-arms of the Commune that have a rampant lion in the middle.

Up above stands the mighty bell cast by Girolamo Santoni of Fano and Giovanni Battista Salvini of Siena in the year 1665 and called by the Sienese « **Campanone** » or « **Sunto** », after the Virgin Mary of the Assumption. The Tower's first clock was the craftsmanship of a certain master Perino (1360) and it was completely re-done by the Jesuit Giovanni of Milan in the year 1425.

The Tower's summit reaches 88 metres high up until the last merlons and, 102 metres up to the top of the lightning conductor. It offers magnificent views of the entire city, the buildings and churches as well as the surrounding hills and the distant Mount Amiata.

The door adjoining the Chapel of the Square leads into the **Podesta Courtyard**, which was constructed in brickwork in 1325 and restored in 1929. This courtyard comprises a porch surmounted by a shelf on which open out a series of a large three-mullioned windows. Along the walls, there are a number of coat-of-arms of the Podesta, a rather damaged and incomplete fresco of the 14th century, depicting the **Madonna and two Angels,** and a statue of the **Mangia.** At the end of the courtyard is the entrance to the Town Theatre of the Revived, which was once the ancient hall of the Republic's Grand Council and, in 1560, adapted by Riccio to serve as a theatre. It was re-done by Bibbiena in 1753, later re-touched and then restored in 1951.

THE INTERIOR – After having visited the exterior of the Palazzo Pubblico, let us step into its interior by going through the portal situated at the right of the Podesta Courtyard, which is formed by an arch decorated with a frieze of foliage and a statue. The fanlight has a bas-relief with two wolves and, in the centre, a rampant crowned lion.

The ground floor of the Palazzo is almost entirely occupied by the Commune's offices. At the end of the initial EN-TRANCE HALL, which keeps in custody the bracelets with tiny bronze bells made by Giacomo Cozzarelli belonging to the Palazzo del Magnifico, on the far left is the entrance to the VESTIBULE that is formed of four spans. Here, one can find on the left wall, two wolves of stone dating from the 14th century, some gargoyles on the eaves attributed to Giovanni Pisano and a **statuette of Moses** by Antonio Federighi. The right wall of the third span bears the fresco by Sano di Pietro of the « **Saintly and Blessed Pietro Alessandrini, Ambrogio Sansedoni and Andrea Gallerani** » (1446). Opening out at the sides of the Vestibule are the following halls: the second on the right, or

MAYORS HALL, has a **Madonna and Child and the Saints John, Michael and Galgano** all by Sodoma (1537), as well as 17th century frescoes on the vault. The third, known as the WAITING ROOM or « OF BICCHERNA », has on the left wall a famous fresco by Sano di Pietro of the **Incoronation of Mary, Angels and the Saints Bernardine and Catherine of Siena** (1445), 17th century frescoes on the vault and, on the right, a marquetry benchcover of the 15th century.

The fourth hall, or SECRETARY GENERALS OFFICE, keeps in custody, situated on the left wall, a **« Resurrection »,** which is a vigorous fresco by Sodoma (1535) and, on the right, a standard by Arcangelo Salimbeni, depicting the **Madonna and St. Sebastian.** Out of the halls situated on the opposite side, the ones worthy of attention are the first that was probably the ancient **Chapel of the Nine,** whose ceiling bears a **Blessed Christ among the cherubs,** work of Simone Martini (perhaps dating 1339), the **Evangelists** by Lorenzo Veneziano, the **Blessed Andrea Gallerani,** Abbott St. Anthony and the **Annunciation** by Andrea Vanni (about 1370). The third and EX-MATRIMONIAL HALL, has in front of it a pillar with an imperial eagle and two frescoed angels by Sodoma, while inside, there is a huge but rather damaged fresco by Vecchietta depicting the **Madonna of the Misericordia and the Saints Bernardine and Michael** (1461).

Hall of the Globe

The Majesty by Simone Martini

THE CIVIC MUSEUM

Once back in the Entrance Hall, let us go up to the first floor that houses the CIVIC MUSEUM. After the Vestibule, where one can view the magnificent She-Wolf by Lorenzo di Turino (1429-30) made of gold-plated tin, that once stood in the square, as well as the remains of a Majesty fresco by Ambrogio Lorenzetti, we enter the great **Hall of the Globe.** This hall takes its name from a huge map depicting the territory of Siena which was painted by Ambrogio Lorenzetti during the early 1300 and which, today, is unfortunately lost forever.

However, even though this 14th century map has disappeared what is left behind is a 14th century of fable and poetry: hanging on the large wall in the background is the corroded and faded tapestry of the MAJESTY by Simone Martini, considered one of the greatest protagonists and creators of 14th century painting. Born, according to tradition, in Siena in 1284 – if we follow Vasari who recalls the artist's death at the age of 60 years in 1344 – Simone painted the Majesty, which is his first certain work, in

1315. But, only six years later, he was forced to restore it because of damage caused by humidity. In the centre, on a filigree gilded throne, the Madonna appears as though embroidered in the precious grain of a very old cloth material; she gazes sweetly ahead, her face so empyreal, composed, immaculate and, yet, transparent and lacking in substance, while a group of angels and saints draw back to look at her.

The overhanging canopy, borne by angels and just lightly blown by a gentle breeze, stands out against the intense and vivid blue sky. It gives a realistic touch to this scene that is so rarefied, as though viewed through a net curtain that fades away into the distance and makes the whole composition appear out of focus. Even though this is a very traditional theme, Simone Martini knew just how to give it a new air and new artistic meaning.

The composition is framed by a wide band of twenty medallions with figures of Christ, prophets and evangelists. Below, in the centre, is a two-faced figure representing the old law and the new, while another medallion reproduces the seal of the Republic.

On the opposite wall is another fresco by Simone Martini depicting **« Guidoriccio da Fogliano, victorious over the castles of Montemassi and Sassoforte of Maremma »,**

which rebelled against Siena in 1328. This fresco, which was done the year following, belonged to a series of representations, unfortunately not in existence today, of the Castles that fell under the rule of the Sienese Republic.

Dominating in the centre is the figure of the army leader who, dignified and reserved amidst the pomp of the parade uniforms, marches triumphantly towards the conquered castles. Without a doubt, this fresco is one of the best and most renowned works ever produced by Martini. In the wide expanse of the scene, where the decorative element so typically Simone acquires monumental greatness against the limpid volumes of the turreted castles that stand out in the background in a barren, deserted landscape, the reality of the event sublimes in a climate of heroic and poetic evocation.

Other paintings decorate the hall: high up on the wall of the arches are two huge monochrome frescoes depicting the VICTORY OF THE SIENESE OVER THE FLORENTINES AT POGGIO IMPERIALE, near Poggibonsi (8th September 1479), by Giovanni di Cristofano and Francesco d'Andrea (1480) and the VICTORY OF THE SIENESE LED BY GIORDANO ORSINI OVER THE ENGLISH « HATTED » COMPANY LED BY NICCOLO' DA MONTEFELTRO AT ASINALUNGA (Sinalunga) or at TORRITA IN VAL DI CHIANA (1363) by Lippo Vanni. On the pillars underneath are depicted, from the right, the **Blessed Andrea Gallerani** and **Ambrogio Sansedoni,** of the 17th century, **St. Catherine of Siena** by Vecchietta (1461), **St. Bernardine** by Sano di Pietro (1460), the **Blessed Bernardo Tolomei** by Sodoma (1533).

Underneath the fresco of Guidoriccio da Fogliano lies a **Madonna and Child** by Guido da Siena, known also as the « Madonna of Guido ». This panel, which is of great importance since it concerns the study of the first witnesses of Sienese painting, is signed and dated 1221, however, more recent critics while recognizing the work's authenticity and originality of the inscription, are unanimous in assigning it to the late 13th century. In the following year, either Duccio or one of his pupils, repainted the head and hands of the Virgin and Baby.

On the right and left of the Majesty is a fresco by Sodoma (1529) depicting two monumental figures of St. Vittore and St. Ansano being baptized.

From the Hall of the Globe, we pass on the right to the **Hall of Peace or of the Nine,** which was once the seat of the Nine-Member Government. The Hall treasures the most famous series of profane frescoes out of all Sienese painting, done by Ambrogio LORENZETTI (Siena, 1319-1348?) and painted between 1337 and 1339. This great representation of a political, didactic and moral theme, is comprised of three parts: « THE ALLEGORY OF GOOD

The effects of good Government (A. Lorenzetti)

The effects of bad Government (A. Lorenzetti)

GOVERNMENT », « THE EFFECTS OF GOOD GOVERNMENT IN THE CITY AND IN THE COUNTRYSIDE », and « THE ALLEGORY AND THE EFFECTS OF BAD GOVERNMENT ». Unfortunately, this composition has suffered much deterioration over the centuries. The Good Government is represented by an old solemn king, clothed in black and white which are the colours of the « **Balzana** » or flag of Siena and of the city's coat-of-arms. On the left of this stand Justice, Moderation and Magnanimity, while on the right are Prudence, Strength and Peace. Up above are the three Biblical Virtues, while at the king's feet lies the she-wolf suckling Aschio and Semio, sons of Remus and the mythical founders of Siena.

On the side are the **Effects of the Good Government,** a pleasant representation of 13th century Siena where, among the towers and merloned buildings, thrive peaceful activities, elegant riding-parties parade up and down and young daning girls throng the city's squares and streets. It is almost a panoramic tale about the everyday events of the city and its characters. Then, there is the bare countryside around Siena; an undulated stretch of mounts and hills dotted with castles, woods, fields as seen by the first artist – from Grecian right up to Roman times – to interpret with brush and paints the emotion and enchantment of true nature. In front of this lies a rather deteriorated fresco of the **Bad Government and its effects** with, on the right, **Tyranny** astride a black goat and seated between **Cruelty, Deception, Defraud, Fury, Discord and Perfidy. Here, Justice** appears chained and trampled upon. Above are **Avarice, Arrogance** and **Vainglory.**

In spite of the allegoric subjects, which dominate majority of the frescoes, and which are certainly not congenial to the artist, the imposing conceptual structure based on the antithesis between the good and the evil, between the good and the bad government of public affairs, is transformed into poetry by way of a language of great originality and a work of great dimensions. And it is in this work that Ambrogio Lorenzetti achieves his artistic ideal, which is expressed in the perfect harmony of all the colours, in the identity of each colour and volume, in the slow movement of the lines that, together, define the entire mass and colour.

From the Hall of Peace we enter into the hall facing us, namely the HALL OF PILLARS, which treasures two paintings by Neroccio di Bartolomeo Landi « **The Sermon of St. Bernardine** » and « **St. Bernardine freeing a woman**

The sermon of St. Bernardino

possessed », that are reproduced on the two sides of a panel. Here one also finds a fresco of the 14th century Sienese school, depicting the **Saints Stephen, Magdalen and Anthony**, an **Annunciation** again of the 14th century and a valuable **Madonna and Child**, by Duccio.

In the centre of the hall is a glass showcase containing a gilded, wooden casket decorated with figures of the Patron Saints of Siena, dating from the late 14th century, a 15th century coffer, the bells of the Church of St. Christopher that sounded the alarm at the Battle of Montaperti, and a wooden casket made by Antonio Barili. Once back in the Hall of the Globe, we pass into the ANTECHAPEL decorated with frescoes by Taddeo di Bartolo (1363-1422) that depict characters from Roman history and Greek-Roman mythology. Also, the fresco on the left wall depicting St. Christopher is by Taddeo di Bartolo, while the wooden statue of San Nicola di Bari on the same wall is by Antonio Federighi.

Lying adjacent to the Antechapel is a magnificent CHAPEL closed off by an elegant wrought-iron and tin-plated gate, which was probably designed by Jacopo della Quercia and made in 1437 by the Sienese smiths Giacomo di Giovanni and his son Giovanni. Inside the chapel is a small suspended holywater stoup decorated with gilded bronze figures by Giovanni di Turino (1434) and a rich Gothic chandelier in gilded and painted wood, dating from 1370.

Chapel of Palazzo Pubblico

The marble altar by Marrina has hanging above it a beautiful panel by Sodoma of the **Holy Family** and **San Leonardo** (1536?), while the vaults over the walls are covered with frescoes by Taddeo di Bartolo, probably done in around 1407 and depicting the Evangelists, the Learned Men of the Church, the various Prophets and the Teachings of the life of the Virgin. Below are the funerals of the Madonna.

Lined up along the Chapel walls are the stalls of the choir, magnificently carved out of wood and, on the stall backs are inlaid wooden panels illustrating the Creed. This work is attributed to Domenico di Nicolò – upon completion of this work he was nicknamed « Domenico of the Choirs » – and was carried out between the years 1415 and 1428. The Choir is considered a true masterpiece of woodcarving technique and high craftsmanship, thanks to the harmony of proposition and to the extraordinary designs of the elegant decorations.

Walking trough the Antechapel and turning right we enter the **Hall of the Cardinals**, on whose walls we can see two frescoes depicting the figures of Saints. Above the entrance is a 14th century Crucifix mounted on a plate, while nearby the dividing pillar is a shrine by Guidoccio Cozzarelli with the **Madonna and Child and Four Angels.** Next to the wall on the right are two plaster-coated wooden statues of St. Anthony the Abbot and St. Ambrose, which are attributed to a follower of Jacopo della Quercia, probably Antonio Federighi.

On the intrados of the door to the « Balia » Hall are fragments of a much larger fresco by Ambrogio Lorenzetti, depicting « Three Saints and the Benefactor genuflecting before them ».

Then we enter, on the left, into the **Hall of the Consistory,** which is adorned with a marble portal by Bernardo Rossellino (1468) and inlaid wooden doors by Niccolò dei Cori. The frescoes of the vault are in pale, radiant colours and narrate **« Heroic episodes of Roman and Greek history according to Valerius the Great ».** Their creator is Domenico Beccafumi, nicknamed Mecarino (1529-35). Lying at the centre of the vault is the figure of Justice flanked by Harmony and Patriotism. Above the portal is the JUDGE-MENT OF SOLOMON, a valuable canvas by Luca Giordano. Instead, on the walls hang three magnificent 18th century tapestries coming from the Gobelins workshop and the patterns are based on the cartoons by Charles Le Brun (The Allegory of the Earth, Wind and Fire). There are also five other smaller tapestries of Florentine handicraft that date from the 16th century.

Retracing our steps back to the Hall of the Cardinals and going through the doorway of the wall facing us, we now enter the **« Balia » Hall or of the Priors.** This hall, which is divided into two sections by an arch, takes its name from the Bench of the Balia Magistrates, who held their meetings in this very hall. The entire hall is adorned with frescoes.

The vaults, right up to the cornice, were painted with frescoes during the period 1407-1408, by the Sienese artist Martino di Bartolomeo. He divided the ceiling into sixteen triangular portions and, in each one, he painted the half-bust of a Virtue. These Virtues, with their soft, femminine figures, vaguely remind one of Ambrogio Lorenzetti's style of painting and perhaps constitute the most beautiful work ever done by this artist.

The arch spanning the hall bears the figures of the **Four Evangelists** and six busts of emperors and warriors, while on the pillars we find other smaller figures of Virtue. The walls and the fanlight above the arch are painted with a vast series of frescoes, carried out in the year 1408 by Spinello di Luca di Arezzo, nicknamed Aretino (about 1346-1410), and depicting the « **Great Deeds of Pontiff Alexander III** », who belonged to the Bandinelli family of Siena, was the animator of the Lombard League and conqueror of Federico Barbarossa. This particular painting is a rare example of this non-Sienese painter's work in

Alexander returning to Rome accompanied by Barbarossa and the Doge of Venice

Siena, however, Aretino was well-known in the city, because right from the year 1404, he was commissioned to paint inside the Cathedral by the Master Caterino di Corsino, Superintendent of the Duomo Trust. These frescoes represent the artist's last important work, in collaboration with his son Parri, who was 20 years of age at the time, and they still belong to the long tradition of 13th century art that is dominated by the figure and work of Giotto.

Starting with the square on the above right, on the wall in front of the window, we find:

Alexander receiving the pontifical crown (above); **He entrusts the sword to the Doge of Venice** (below).

On the other half of the wall we have:

The founding of the city of Alexandria (above); **Barbarossa submitting himself to the Pope** (below).

The fanlight on the following wall facing the entrance door shows:

Alexander pardoning Prince Otto (right); **The Canonization of the Danish King Canute.**

Along the entire lower half of the wall we find:

Alexander returning to Rome accompanied by Barbarossa and the Doge of Venice.

The wall with the windows bears:

A German Ambassador handing a message to the King of Francia, seated near the Pope (right); **The Doge presents the captive Prince Otto to Alexander** (left).

The fanlights of the entrance wall:

Conversation with Ludwig VII, King of France (left); **Alexander abandons Rome disguised as a Carthusian** (right).

Along the entire lower part of the wall:

The Venetian fleet defeats that of Barbarossa at Punta Salvore.

The fanlight of the arch over the entrance door depicts:

The Antipope Victor IV being crowned in the presence of Barbarossa (left); **Alexander receiving gifts at Ninfa** (right). Near the exit door:

The Lateran Synod (left); **The Four Antipopes condemned to the stake** (right).

The hall on the right has a beautiful wooden door, the work of Domenico di Niccolò (or « Domenico of the Choirs »), while the wooden counter placed along the length of the entrance hall, is the work of Barna di Turino. From the landing we enter the **Hall of the Risorgimento,** painted with frescoes by Sienese and Tuscan artists of the late 19th century: Pietro Aldi, Giorgio Bandini, Amos Cassioli, Alessandro Franchi, Cesare Maccari, Gaetano Marinelli and many others. The extremely valuable paintings represent the decisive historical events leading to the Unification of Italy and the main characters who, together with King Victor Emanuel II, took part in them.

Placed around the hall are marble statues and busts of

political and artistic personalities of the 19th century, sculptured by Enea Becheroni, Emilio Gallori, Arnaldo Prunai, Tito Sarocchi and others.

The door on the left leads to the five halls which encircle the Podestà Courtyard and which treasure the Civic Museum's other collections with art works of smaller dimensions. In the first hall, the glass showcases contain Sienese ceramics and majolica dating from the 15th to the 17th century, crafts, bronzes and an extremely rare collection of merchant tesserae dating from the Middle Ages. The walls are decorated with paintings of the Sienese school and others. Instead, the halls numbering second to the fifth contain a rich numismatic collection arranged in the order of CORPUS NUMMORUM ITALICORUM and comprising very rare coins of Populonia, coins and seals of the Roman era, more than 6000 medieval coins, 1500 medals from Renaissance times to the present day and, a precious collection of medieval seals. 16th and 17th century paintings adorn the walls of these above-mentioned halls.

Climbing up the great staircase and turning to the left after the first flight of steps, we arrive at those halls of the Museum containing the plaster casts of important works, among which the casts of the portal of San Petronio in Bologna and the famous Sepulchre of Ilaria del Carretto in Lucca by Jacopo della Quercia. Continuing up the stairs, we come to the **Loggia,** which overlooks the Piazza del Mercato (market square) and which offers a fantastic view of the valley and the Eastern ramifications of the city. The original sculptures by Jacopo della Quercia, which belong to the Gaia Fountain, are kept here and although eroded over the centuries, these sculptures still display the masterly style and great skill of the artist.

The wall facing the entrance has a beautiful fresco by Ambrogio Lorenzetti, depicting the Madonna and Child (1340).

From the Loggia we pass into the **Great Hall of the Lords,** now the Town Council. Here we find two canvases by Amos Casisoli, the « **Oath of Pontida** » and « **Provenzan Salvani in Siena's Campo Square** ». This latter painting relates the story of how Provenzan Salvani was so desperately in need of money to release his friend Vigna, who was held captive by Emperor Charles V, that he « made his body shake through to the veins » – as quoted by Dante in Purgatorio – and was reduced to begging for alms in Campo Square.

The paintings on the vault, which depict Sienese tales, are all done by artists of the late 16th century.

The other halls on the 2nd floor boast a rich collection of prints, among which quite a few by Jacques Callot and Stefano della Bella, paintings of the 17th and 18th centuries, portraits of famous Sienese personages, geographical maps and interesting documents about Siena, the history of her topography and town-planning over the centuries, and the famous Palio festival.

Lying above the Council halls and those of the prints is the topmost floor, also known as the « MARCOLINA », which is under renovation in line with plans for the Museum's extension. Since 1973, this floor hosts a large fresco by Sodoma depicting the Madonna, Saints and the Eternal Father (1539), the remnants of which were detached from the Chapel of the Square.

THE CAMPO SQUARE

Out of the Palazzo Pubblico (Town Hall) we find ourselves once again in the famous Campo Square, adorned with a series of beautiful buildings that all go to form a complex of town-planning whose planimetrical layout, functionality and space appear closely conditioned by the architecture of the buildings. The CAMPO was under the continuous care of the town authorities, long before they had their headquarters established here.

The severe statuary regulations of 1309, by which the construction of galleries, awnings and projections on the facades overlooking the square were abolished and even the windows had to be either mullioned or three-mullioned, were not enacted solely to maintain a certain dignity of the square but also to reaffirm the value of it being a luminous oasis opening out below, coming into contact with the unlimited space of the valley underneath, where the narrow arteries of the city's three districts converge. In many cases these rules concerning the windows were not respected, however, this did not spoil the harmony and beauty of the whole.

THE STATE ARCHIVES

We now start the visit round the square beginning from the side of the Chapel of the Square and, straightaway, on the right hand side at the corner of Via Rinaldini, we are confronted with the imposing PALAZZO PICCOLOMINI. Construction work was started in the year 1469 – probably according to Bernardo Rossellino's project – and it was built by Pietro Paolo Porrina. This building is considered the most beautiful and significant example of Sienese Renaissance architecture. Its lines, which are very similar to those of the Florentine Palazzo Ruccellai by Leon Battista Alberti and Palazzo Piccolomini in Pienza by the same Rossellino, have that composure and elegance often found in the best Florentine Renaissance architecture. Palazzo Piccolomini consists of two floors divided and emphasized by elegant cornices. The whole surface is covered in smooth ashlar and divided symetrically by two series of elegant and simple mullioned windows.

Ornamental loops in wrought-iron and coats-of-arms adorn the building.

The Palazzo Piccolomini houses the **State Archives** that were established in 1775 and later put in order in 1885. These archives comprise a vast collection of documents of vital importance to those interested in knowing the political, civil and artistic life of Siena and the entire region. There are over 60,000 parchments dating from 736, which relate to resolutions and statutes of the Republic, correspondence and action taken by the financial and judicial authorities.

The most interesting part of the whole collection is arranged in three different halls. There are documents relating to events and characters recalled by Dante in his Divine Comedy; Imperial Charters and Papal Bulls, Giovanni Boccaccio's will, autographs and letters of famous men, women and artists; documents concerning the execution of renowned works such as the Majesty by Duccio, Fonte Gaia and Pergamo by Nicola Pisano. There are also papers of a commercial nature on Sienese studies, on the Medici family, on the city's siege and surrender, on the Palio, as well as an interesting collection of illuminated statutes

Circumcision of Jesus (Lippo Vanni - 1357)

namely the « Caleffo dell'Assunta » by Niccolò di Ser Sozzo Tegliacci (1334) and the « Trading Statute », illuminated by Sano di Pietro in 1472. The famous collection of the **« Biccherna Plates »**, of notable historic and artistic value, are reproduced here by courtesy of the Ministry for cultural affairs and the environment and the State Archives. This collection is comprised of painted plates used half-yearly to cover the Accounts Ledgers of the Biccherna and Gabella administrations. The two authorities, who were responsible for the main finance offices of the Republic, were renewed every six months and at the end of each administrative term they had painted on the wooden cover of the accounts ledgers the coat-of-arms and the members of the administration, as well as a sacred or symbolic scene to record the most important event of that period. The plates that date from 1268 to 1659, were painted by some of the most renowned masters of the era, such as **Ambrogio** and **Pietro Lorenzetti, Giovanni di Paolo, Vecchietta, Sano di Pietro, Francesco di Giorgio Martini, Neroccio di Bartolomeo Landi, Domenico Beccafumi** to name a few.

Tax-collector and traxpayer (Ascribed to A. Lorenzetti - 1340)

Mystic nuptials of the Saints Catherine of Alessandria and Catherine from Siena (D. Beccafumi - 1548)

The restaured Government keeps in check the citizens (Unknown author - 1385)

Apart from the Biccherna plates, the Archives also hold others belonging to the ledgers of St. Mary's Hospital and various other Sienese authorities.

After Palazzo Piccolomini, at the beginning of the square's semicircle and just past Via Rinaldini, rises up **Palazzo Chigi-Zondadari,** which is a very ancient building that was later rebuilt in 1724 by Antonio Valeri. Then follows **Palazzo Sansedoni** which, with its size, its tower that once stood tall and overpowering, its curved form in line with the Campo Square, resembles very closely the Palazzo Pubblico. Even the series of elegant three-mullioned windows perfectly harmonizes with the entire architectural complex of the Campo.

The building's construction dates from the year 1216; it was, however, extended and transformed in 1339 by Agostino di Giovanni. The original facade overlooking Banchi di Sopra can be reconstructed from a beautiful design by Giovanni d'Agostino (1339), whilst the one looking onto the Campo is the result of an extension made in the 18th century, when the whole aggregation of buildings dating from the early 1200 that were re-done and extended as mentioned in 1339, was transformed into one high-class residential quarter. The interior hosts many frescoes on the ceilings by Gian Domenico Ferretti (1745-60).

Among Vicolo San Paulo and San Pietro we come up against the rear facade of the Loggia di Mercanzia, re-done in 1763 according to the designs of Ferdinando Fuga, then there are the De Metz houses and, beyond Costarella dei Barbieri, is the Palazzo d'Elci, which is a merloned building of the 1500. And beyond this point opens up the rowdy and characteristic **Chiasso del Bargello** (alley of the Police Headquarters).

ITINERARY 2

Palazzo Chigi-Saracini - Piazza del Duomo - The Cathedral - The New Cathedral - The Metropolitan Opera Museum - The Baptistry - The Archibishops Palace - The Church of Santa Maria della Scala.

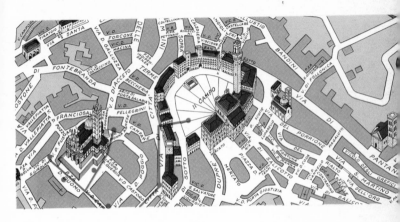

PALAZZO CHIGI-SARACINI – Now we leave, even though a little sadly, the magic of the sound-scene of Campo, with its elegant shell of red brickwork and climbing up through Vicolo San Pietro and then Costarella dei Barbieri we arrive in Via di Città, where our gaze meets the gentle curved form of PALAZZO CHIGI-SARACINI that stands at number 89.

As always here in Siena, the harshness of the stone is softened by the red brickwork of the upper floors, the wide three-mullioned windows, which dig out proportionate hollows in the solid mass of the wall, in a fusion of majesty and decorative charm so typical of this architecture.

The Palazzo, once called MARESCOTTI and whose construction was begun in the 12th century, was completed in the early 14th century, however, in successive centuries, it underwent quite a number of restorations. The building is flanked on the left hand side by a tower, from where Cerreto Ceccolini is reputed to have followed the stages of the Battle of Montaperti giving the Sienese up-to-date reports on the action taking place.

In 1932, on the request of Count Guido Chigi-Saracini, the Palazzo became the seat of the **Chigi Music Academy** which in a short space of time came to be considered

43

the most important academy for the perfection of musical studies.

The « Sienese Music Week » is held here every year in July and attracts concert musicians, music lovers and singers from all over the world. The dark entrance that leads onto the picturesque courtyard takes us into the Palazzo's interior, which is of extraordinary beauty for its priceless furnishings, the interesting music halls and their rich collections of musical instruments and for the great quantity of art works that are of considerable value.

Apart from the luminous Concert Hall, furnished in a severe 18th century style and with the fresco on the vault by Viligiardi depicting the RETURN FROM THE BATTLE OF MONTAPERTI, the GALLERIA is also of great interest with its valuable art works dating from the 14th century, the Renaissance period and the 17th century. To name a few:

the Madonna and Child, a marble bas-relief attributed by many to Donatello or Vecchietta; the **Deposition,** a coloured wooden statue, and a **Sketch for the Gaia Fountain,** both by Jacopo della Quercia; a painted **Crucifix** of the Berlinghieri school; another painted **Crucifix** of the Giotto school; **St. Paul** by Simone Martini; the **Three Magi,** the **Madonna and St. John, St. Martin,** the **Madonna and Four Saints,** all by Sassetta; the **Madonna and Child** by Matteo di Giovanni; the **Madonna and Child** by Neroccio di Bartolomeo; the **Madonna and Child with Two Angels,** a fantastic masterpiece by Botticelli; the **Madonna in adoration** of **Baby Jesus** by Perugino; the **Madonna and Child** by Pinturicchio; the **Madonna and Child** by Pontormo; a **Knight** by Sebastiano del Piombo; the **Holy Family** by Cima da Conegliano; **Figures of Monks.**

There are also works by Sodoma, Beccafumi, artists of the Leonardo school, Brescianino, Peruzzi and other Renaissance artists of the following period.

Farther on we come to PALAZZO PICCOLOMINI or DELLE PAPESSE, which today is the headquarters of the Bank of Italy. It was commissioned by Caterina Piccolomini, the sister of Pope Pius II, in the late 15th century (1460-1495), probably according to the designs of Bernardo Rossellino.

The building, which has undergone much restoration work, such as that carried out in 1804 by Augusto Corbi, is in the Renaissance style, with its characteristic facade of rough ashlar below and smooth ashlar above. However, what detaches the building from this style, as is the case with nearly all the 15th century Sienese buildings compared to the Florentine ones, is the adoption of artistic elements taken from other styles and, in particular, from the Gothic style. For this building, and this can be applied even to the others, has two orders of mullioned windows decorating the upper floors.

At the corner of Via di Città and Via del Castoro, stands **Palazzo Marsili**, all brick, built in 1444 on the site of an even older building by Luca di Bartolo di Bagnacavallo and restored by Giuseppe Partini in 1876. Even though in full Renaissance, the building preserves Gothic elements as displayed by the three orders of mullioned windows that open up the facade. Leaving Via del Castoro on the right, we carry on along Via di Città until Piazza Postierla, where **Casatorre Forteguerri stands;** opposite is a column bearing the marble figure of the Sienese She-Wolf (1487) and an elegant flagmast in wrought-iron dating from the 15th century.

We then enter Via del Capitano where, at number 1, stands the **Palazzo Chigi alla Postierla,** once Piccolomini-Adami, of noble 16th century architecture attributed to Riccio. This building has two halls housing frescoes by the Flemish painter Bernard Van Rantwyck and stuccoes by Marcello Sparti of Urbino (1573). In the same street, at number 15, stands the **Palazzo del Capitano del Popolo** (Building of the Governor of the People), so-called because it is the headquarters of the Chief Justice. Later this Palazzo belonged first to the Grottanelli family, then to the Pecci and, finally, to the Piccolomini family. It dates from the late 1200 to the early 1300 and is typically Gothic as can be seen by the Sienese arches below and the mullioned windows of the upper floors.

Via del Capitano leads us directly into PIAZZA DEL DUOMO and the best view of the whole square can be had from the left hand corner at the end of the street. The long facade of the St. Mary of the Scala Hospital, the Archibishop's Palace, the huge arcades of the New Cathedral, the Prefecture and, most of all, the grand proportions of the Cathedral, which should not be considered a mere result or synthesis of the various architectural currents that flowed through Siena and which contributed towards qualifying it certain characteristics and aspects, but instead should be seen as being a substantially new creation, in virtue of which and for the very first time, the artistic culture of Siena came to the forefront with a certain authority and took on the role of protagonist of that era.

THE DUOMO

The story of the erection of the Duomo is long and complicated. It is considered one of the most famous and richest Cathedrals of Europe, although little is known of the very first events of this illustrious building and the few documents in existence, relating to the original project and the construction of the oldest parts, have unfortunately raised certain doubts and left a number of questions unanswered. It is presumed that the construction work was started on a plateau that extended adjacent to the most ancient nucleus of the city, namely Castelvecchio and, where once stood though in a different position the very old church. The first certain evidence dates from 1136, at which time during a special delegation of citizens, the St. Mary Organization, the erection of the Duomo was commissioned and financed entirely by the Town Municipality. In 1258, the administration was handed to the Monks of the San Galgano Abbey, who kept this office almost continuously right up to the year 1314. It is, therefore, highly improbable that, and as is often asserted, the Duomo of Siena was dependent upon the famous Cirstercian Abbey, which, above other things, was only begun in 1220 when the Duomo was already well under way in its construction.

In 1265, it was decided that the interior be done because in September of that same year the Superintendent Brother Melano, converted by the Cistercian Monks of San Galgano, went especially to Pisa and made a contract with NICOLA PISANO. The latter's very first work and the most treasured of all the works carried out in the church, was the pulpit. But even before this era, sculptors of Pisano's circle had already worked in the Duomo, mainly on the grand decorated capitals among which the style of Arnolfo di Cambio can be clearly identified.

In 1284, the Sienese turned to Nicola Pisano's son, Giovanni, to substitute the old and rather simple front with a new and majestic facade. Giovanni Pisano remained in Siena until 1296 and directed the operation of the facade's lower half. However, he was unable to see what was to be a masterpiece of his genius both as a sculptor and architect, for probably on account of contrasting opinions with the Monastery Superintendency he decided to abandon Siena in 1296. After his departure, work on the facade continued though lacking in enthusiasm and, just after the first decade of the 14th century, the project was suspended. In the meanwhile, the building was terminated and comprised of three naves, the apse and the bell-tower. At the same time, the Sienese, who were at the height of their power and wealth, began thinking of extending the Duomo at the Choir end towards Vallepiatta.

The chroniclers of the era record that this extension was started in 1316-1317 amidst much argument and opposition. Then, in 1325 it was decided to bolt the doors of the Baptistry, which stood at the lower end of Vallepiatta – the site of the Duomo's extension – and above the Church, work was already under way on the walls of the Choir when the Sienese devised a new, daring design. On August 23rd, 1339, the « Grand Council of the Republic » decided to extend the Cathedral even further, by creating a longitudinal body with three naves inserted perpendicularly to the South-East flank of the already existing Church. In this way, the old Duomo would form the transept of the new one. The supervision of the building work was assigned to Lando di Pietro, goldsmith, sculptor and engineer and, on the latter's death in August 1340, Giovanni d'Agostino was chosen to carry on the work on the new Duomo and

he proved a very able substitute. However, the Plague broke out in 1348 causing all the work to be suspended and, later in 1355, the entire project was abandoned also because of the evident and irreparable deficiencies in the statics of both the project as well as the construction. Once having demolished the unsafe parts, all efforts were put to completing the old Duomo. Between 1356 and 1359, the vaults were covered under the supervision of Domenico d'Agostino who, in 1350, succeeded his brother. It is to him and not to Jacopo di Mino del Pellicciaio that we should also attribute the facade of the Baptistry; a beautiful design on parchment is preserved in the Trust Museum. In 1377, Giovanni Cecco commenced work on the completion of the facade. Even though the numerous interruptions and extensions have left their mark on the planimetrical lay out as well as on the Cathedral's structure and decorations, the wonderful mass of marble presents an admirable aesthetic unity thanks to the surprising harmony of the Gothic elements, that are more evident on the exterior, and the Romanesque features predominating the Cathedral's interior.

THE EXTERIOR

The Facade – The light and majestic facade, in white marble and with a delicate polychromy obtained from the rose-coloured Sienese stone and the dark green Prato quality, forms the most richly ornamented feature of the entire construction. The theme of the sculpture was dedicated to the glorification of the Virgin, from her preparation right to the advent of Mary: the lower part of the facade depicts stories from the Old Testament up until the ascension into Heaven of the Virgin Mary, while the upper part depicts stories from the New Testament. But today, with the changes that have been made in the order of the statues, this concept is less evident. As we mentioned earlier, the facade can be divided into two parts. The lower one is the work of Giovanni Pisano and his school and features three wide portals splayed and surmounted by triangular-shaped cusps. In spite of the Gothic nature of the decorations, with their delicate leaves, flowers, putti and gargoyles, they also reveal a taste of Romanesque and a great sensitiveness on the part of the sculptor, in the intense play of chiaroscuro on the modelled profiles, the projections and the deep recesses.

The fanlights bear inlaid decorations, while bas-reliefs adorn the walls between the door and architrave, in the centre, and between the architrave and arch, at the sides. The bas-relief on the central doorway is attributed to Tino di Camaino and depicts the « Story of Ann and Joachim ». The side pillars, that continue along the upper part, were designed by Giovanni Pisano. The whole of the immense, high wall is dramatically animated with the STATUES sculptured by Giovanni Pisano and his school, that jut out from the brackets and cornices. Today, the original statues can be seen in the Metropolitan Trust Museum, where they were transferred to save them from deteriorating with time.

The main doorway in bronze, work of the sculptor Enrico Manfini (1958), is dedicated entirely to the Virgin Mary and depicts episodes of her life, characters from the Old Testament, pontifices, saints and artists who contributed to the glorification of Mary.

A cornice by Giovanni di Cecco divides the lower and upper halves and is considered the clearest and most famous example of that florid Gothic style, which with Lorenzo Maitani had already found its greatest success in the Duomo of Orvieto. This part of the facade, which somehow did not fit in perfectly with the underlying section of the portals, stands out for its eminent pictorial qualities obtained by the intense chiaroscuro technique of the dark loggias, the niche surrounded by tabernacles and the inner hollows of the towers.

The facade terminates in three cusps covered in the central part with mosaics done in 1877 by Veneziano Castellani.

They depict:
the **Presentation of Mary** - left cusp;
the **Incoronation of Mary** - central cusp;
tne **Manger scene** - right cusp.

Underneath the central cusp is a huge stained-glass rose-window depicting the « Last Supper », which was designed by Perin del Vaga.

Situated around the rose-window are thirty-six bust statues of Patriarchs and Prophets and, in the four triangles formed by the rose-window and by the panel framing it, are those of the Evangelists.

At the centre of the uppermost part of the panel is a « Madonna ». The original sculptures, dating from the 14th century, by Corbella, are kept in the Metropolitan Trust Museum and were substituted with reproductions made by Tito Sarrocchi and Leopoldo Maccari in the 19th century. The Angel at the top of the highest cusp is the work of Tommaso Redi (1639).

THE SIDES OF THE CATHEDRAL — The whole right side is scanned with pillars and high Gothic windows and, along the entire length are longitudinal stripes of polycrome marble, which are deeply coloured compared with the dichromic facade. This marble decoration covers all the remaining sides of the Cathedral. Extending from this right side is the remaining unfinished part of the New Duomo.

The left side. instead, cannot be viewed because it has been incorporated in the structure of the Archbishop's Palace.

THE BELL-TOWER — It was erected in 1313 over the already existing Bisdomini-Forteguerri tower, designed by Agostino di Giovanni and Agnolo di Ventura, and is in the Romanesque Lombard-Pisan style. It is decorated with dichromic marble placed horizontally to create a continuous series of black and white stripes matching the rest of the church. The tower is opened by six windows that range from the plain mullioned to the eight-mullioned type, and terminates in a cusp formed by a polygon-based pyramid and by other smaller and slender pyramids situated at the sides.

THE DOME — The dome has a hexagonal base, supported by two overlapping orders of galleries. The lower one is enclosed by slender, narrow arches on double columns, whilst the higher one has wide, rounded arches. It is covered with strong ribs and is surmounted by a polygon-shaped lantern.

THE INTERIOR

The interior is in the form of a Latin cross with three naves, and its severe, suggestive grandeur is emphasized further by the chiaroscuro effect of the black and white marble stripes of the walls and pillars. And here the colour is the dominating factor. the vertical line of the pillars is in fact shorted by the horizontal striped decoration and sinks the perspective in a succession of floors, creating a picturesque patterned effect of elegant colours so typical of Siena.

Over the centuries the internal topography and decorations underwent numerous changes: the Duomo's present aspect started to take shape only in 1506, thanks to Pandolfo Petrucci, when the Presbytery was pushed to the back and lowered, the side altars were re-touched and various art works were substituted. A cornice running along the whole perimeter of the main nave, bears one hundred and seventy-two sculptures of Pontifices dating from the 1400 to 1500. Underneath are arranged thirty-six busts of Emperors.

The Flooring – The Cathedral flooring is without a doubt among the most interesting and valuable works. It is a graffito or inlaid decoration that was carried out in successive periods. In fact, it was begun in 1372 and completed only in 1562. The different periods of work

PAVEMENT OF CATHEDRAL

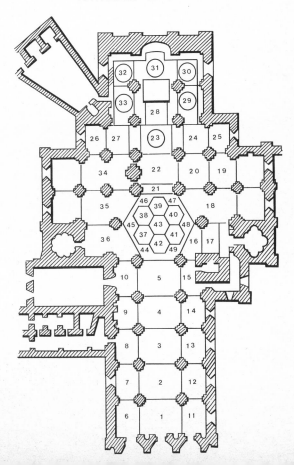

are clearly visible not only because of the artists various styles but, also, and principally because the technique employed was a different one on each occasion. The oldest graffiti consist of a reproduction of engraved designs on marble slabs. The engraved parts were then covered over by a black plasterer's putty to enhance the design. This is the most treasured part of the flooring, and it is generally kept covered and displayed for a month only, during the period 15th August to 15th September.

Later on, another technique was adopted, whereby the design were reproduced on a dark background in such a way as to make them stand out. Later still, the inlaid mosaic system was adopted utilizing coloured marbles. The tour starts from the wall of the entrance, right until the area where the naves cross over the transept.

The median nave flooring:

1) **Hermes Trismegistus,** Giovanni di Stefano (1488); 2) **Coat-of-arms of Siena, Pisa, Lucca, Florence, Arezzo, Orvieto, Rome, Perugia, Viterbo, Massa, Grosseto, Volterra and Pistoia**; 3) **The Imperial Eagle** (1373); 4) **Fortune,** by Paolo Mannucci according to Pinturicchio's designs (1504-1506); 5) **Fortune and Four Philosophers.**

The left nave flooring:

6) **Sibyl of Libya**, Guidoccio Cozzarelli (1483); 7) **Sibyl of Hellesponto**, Neroccio di Bartolomeo Landi (1483); 8) **Sibyl of Phrygia**, Urbano da Cortona (1483); 9) **Sibyl of Samos**, Matteo di Giovanni (1483); 10) **Sibyl of the Albunea or Tiburtine**, Benvenuto di Giovanni (1483).

The right nave flooring:

11) **Sibyl of Delphi**, Urbano da Cortona (1482); 12) **Sibyl of Cumae**, Urbano da Cortona (1482); 13) **Sibyl of Cumae,** Giovanni di Stefano (1482).

In this picture, the artist was inspired by the initial verses of the IV Bucolic of Virgil, quoted on the above right: « Ultima Cumai venit iam carminis aetas; magnus ab integro saeculorum nascitur ordo. Iam redit et Virgo, redeunt Saturinia regna; iam nova progenies caelo demittitur alta ».

14) **Sibyl of Eritrea,** Antonio Federighi (1482); 15) **Sibyl of Persia**, Urbano da Cortona (1483).

The right transept flooring:

16) **The Seven Years of Man**, the original by Antonio Federighi (1475); 17) **Faith, Hope, Charity and Religion,** the original by Domenico Beccafumi; re-make by Alessandro Franchi (1870); 18) **Victory of Jefte over the Ammonites,** Bastiano di Francesco (1482); 19) **Death of Absalom,** Pietro del Minella (1447); 20) **The Emperor Siegmund on the throne**, Domenico di Bartolo (1434).

The presbytery flooring:
21) **Moses makes the water gush forth from the rocks**, Domenico Beccafumi (1525); 22) **Worshipping of the golden calf**, Domenico Beccafumi (1522); 23) **The Psalmist David, David throwing the stone, Goliath hit**, all by Domenico di Niccolò (1423); 24) **Moses**, Paolo di Martino (1426); 25) **Samson's victory over the Philistines**, Paolo di Martino (1426); 26) **Joshua**, Domenico di Niccolò (1426); 27) **Joshua's victory over the King of the Amorrei**, Paolo di Martino (1426); 28) **Abraham's Sacrifice**, Domenico Beccafumi (1546); 29) **Prudence**, Marquis d'Adamo and helpers (1380); 30) **Temperance**, Marquis d'Adamo and helpers (1380); 31) **Misericordia**, Marquis d'Adamo (1406); 32) **Justice**, Marquis d'Adamo (1406). The picture is of great beauty and probably reproduced a design by Ambrogio Lorenzetti. 33) **Fortitude**, Marquis d'Adamo (1406).

Sibyl of Samos (Matteo di Giovanni - 1483)

Massacre of Innocents (Matteo di Giovanni - 1481)

The left transept flooring:
34) **Judith beheads Holophernes and fighting at the gates of Bethune**, Antonio Federighi (1473); 35) **Massacre of Innocents**, Matteo di Giovanni (1481); 36) **Herod usurped of the throne**, Benvenuto di Giovanni (1484).

Flooring underneath the dome:
The panels are all attributed to Domenico Beccafumi, though they were partly re-done by Alessandro Franchi: 37) **Death of Ahab**; 38) **Elijah's Sacrifice**; 39) **Ahab's Sacrifice**; 40) **Killing of the false prophets**; 41) **Scolding of Elijah**; 42) **Elijah ascends into Heaven**; 43) **Pact between Elijah and Ahab.**

In the rhombic shapes framing the abovementioned pictures are:
44) **Elijah resuscitates the widow's son**; 45) **Elijah anoints Jehu**; 46) **Ardia conducts Ahab to Elijah**; 47) **Elijah orders Ardia to bring Ahab to him**; 48) **Elijah nourished by the deer**; 49) **Elijah asks the widow for bread.**

The inner facade – The median portal has bas-reliefs on the pedestals by Urbano da Cortona (1483), which depict stories of Mary. Instead, the two richly decorated columns are the work of Giovanni di Stefano. In the architrave are 15th century bas-reliefs depicting the « **Stories of St. Ansano** ». Nearby the entrance, in the vicinity of two pillars, one on the right and the other on the left, stand two Holy-water stoups by Antonio Federighi.

The right nave – Tucked away in a niche nearby the inner facade is a statue of Pius X, by Fulvio Signorini dating from 1605.

1st altar - **San Gaetano**, by Domenico Canuti;

2nd altar - **Ecstasy of San Girolamo,** by Annibale Mazzuoli (1671);

3rd altar - **Ecstasy of San Francesco of Sales**, by Raffaele Vanni (1654);

4th altar - **Mystic marriage of Santa Caterina,** by Pier Dandini.

Towards the end of the nave, on the right hand side, is the door of the bell-tower flanked by « **Six Scenes from the Life of Mary** » by Urbano da Cortona, and surmounted by the Tomb of the Bishop Tommaso Piccolomini del Testa, work of Neroccio (1484-85). We now arrive to the left part underneath the DOME, which was built between the years 1259 and 1264. It has a hexagonal base and is supported by six pillars, two of which have attached to them the two flagpoles belonging to the « **Carroccio** » (horse-drawn cart bearing the city standard) that was used at the Battle of Montaperti.

There are six columns in the corners each bearing a gilded statue of a saint, the work of Ventura Tiparilli and Bastiano di Francesco. Above these are shell-shaped niches that transform the hexagon into a dodecagon, along which runs a gallery divided by 42 small columns again with the figures of patriarchs and prophets and painted in 1481 by Guidoccio Cozzarelli, Benvenuto di Giovanni and Pellegrino di Mariano.

The right transept – This arm of the transept, like the one on the left, has a double nave separated by composite pillars.

Opening up on the right is the CHAPEL TO THE MADONNA OF THE VOW or CHIGI. It was commissioned by Pope Alexander II and constructed following the designs of Gian Lorenzo Bernini during the period 1655-1661. The architecture, the marble and bronze decorations as well as the gilding of the dome are all significant examples of the Baroque style that reigned in the 17th century. Below is a list of some of the Chapel's most outstanding works:

– **the Madonna of the Vow,** a 13th century plate made by the Guido da Siena school;
– **the Statues of Angels,** by Bernini placed around the Madonna of the Vow;
– **St. Girolamo and St. Mary,** two more statues by Bernini that lie near the entrance.

On the left hand side of the same altar is a canvas by Carlo Maratta, entitled « **Visitation of the Madonna to St. Elizabeth** » and opposite this is a mosaic depicting the « **Flight into Egypt** », taken from a painting of the same theme again by Maratta.

Coming out from the Chapel, on the right of the transept, we are faced with a seated statue of **Alexander III** by Antonio Raggi (1663); on the altar opposite is **San Bernardino** by Mattia Preti; on the left hand side stands the statue of Alexander VII by Ercole Ferrata (1668); then we come to the **Chapel of the Holy Sacrament** where we can view five interesting bas-reliefs depicting the « **Four Evangelists** » by Giovanni Francesco of Imola and « **St. Paul** » by Giovanni di Turino. Nearby the altar is the « **Adoration of the Shepherds** » by Alessandro Casolani (1594).

The Presbytery – The main altar, which is the work of Baldassare Peruzzi (1532), is decorated with a huge bronze ciborium by Vecchietta (1467-72) that once belonged to the Church of the St. Mary of the Servants Hospital. It was brought here in 1506 and took the place of the Majesty by Duccio that was transferred to the Trust Museum. Standing at the sides are two candlesticks in the form of Angels by Giovanni di Stefano (1489), while the other two angels below are the exceptional masterpieces of Francesco di Giorgio Martini (1497-99). The pillars sustain eight Angels by Beccafumi (1548-50) and, facing them above are two chancels, the one on the right sculptured by Antonio Barili and that on the left sculptured according to the designs of Riccio (1550),

The main altar (Baldassare Peruzzi - 1532)

The Apse – The niche was, at one time, adorned with frescoes by Beccafumi, but today, all that remains are the restored or repainted parts of Paradise, some Apostles (1544); underneath is the Assumption by Bartolomeo Casi (1594) and at the sides are frescoes by Ventura Salimbeni depicting Esther and Ahasuerus on the right, the Hebrews in the Desert on the left, and at the far ends are figures of Saints. Lying up above is a valuable circular stained-glass window that was made in 1288 following cartoons by Duccio di Buoninsegna. This window, which is the oldest of its type in Italy, depicts **Death**, the **Assumption and Incoronation of the Virgin**, the **Four Evangelists** and the **Four Patron Saints of Siena**.

The apse houses the great choir carved out of wood that occupies the lower part of the niche and runs across the entire length of the three naves. It was started in 1363 and finished in 1397 and, originally, it comprised over ninety stalls arranged in double rows, surmounted by canopies and decorated with tabernacles and statues of saints. The parts flanking the niche are all that remain today of this splendid 13th century complex, inlaid by Francesco and Jacopo del Tonghio. The wonderful panels applied to the stall backs are the work of Brother Giovanni of Verona: they were made for the choir of the Convent of San Benedetto at Porta Tufi and were installed in the Cathedral Choir in 1503. These panels are painted with beautiful still-life pictures and views of the city. The majestic main stalls, Renaissance in style, were instead inlaid by Teseo Bartolini of Pienza and Benedetto di Giovanni of Montepulciano, and designed by Riccio in the late 16th century.

We enter the **Sacristy** from the left hand side of the Presbytery and the entrance door is adorned with a suspended holy-water stoup made of gilded bronze and white enamelled marble that is considered a true masterpiece of Giovanni di Turino's craftsmanship (1437).

From the Vestibule, with its bronze bust of Alexander VII that was sculptured by Melchiorre Caffà, we pass into the CAPITULARY HALL, which is decorated with the portraits of the Pontefices and Bishops of Siena. At the end of the hall is a painting of the « **Madonna and Child with the Saints Sebastiano and Rocco** », which is attributed to Giacomo Pacchiarotti and, at the sides are two panels by Sano di Pietro: one depicting « **St. Bernardine giving a Sermon in Piazza del Campo** » (1430) and the other of « **St. Bernardine in Piazza San Francesco** » (1440).

These paintings take on particular importance because they portray the architecture of the buildings as they were in the 15th century.

Hanging on the left wall is a painting of St. Bernardine, again by Sano di Pietro.

The left transept – Standing next to the dome pillars is the famous **Pulpit** sculptured by NICOLA PISANO, aided by his son Giovanni and the pupils Arnolfo di Cambio, Donato and Lapo di Ricevuto, in the years (1266-68).

The pulpit is of a slightly later period than the equally famous one in the Duomo of Pisa, however it displays an impressive evolution in style. Compared to the aristocratic and detached composure of the figures on the Pisan pulpit, to the simplicity of its perspective and to the solemnity of the scenes depicted, this Sienese pulpit possesses a greater power of expression, a freer and more complex type of sculpture and the characters depicted appear more alive and dramatic in their actions.

The pulpit is supported by nine columns, made of granite, porphyry and green marble, that are placed alternately on pedestals and on bases in the shape of lions or

Pulpit by Nicola Pisano

Massacre of Innocents

lionesses clawing at animals. Instead, the main column rests on a group sculpture representing the seven liberal arts, i.e. Grammar, Dialectics, Rhetoric, Philosophy, Arithmetic, Geometry, Astronomy and Music.

Above the columns and Corinthian capitals, the arches span in an elegant trefoiled pattern. Between each of the arches and resting on the capitals is a statue of Virtue. The whole upper wall of the pulpit is divided into seven panels that are separated by statues of Prophets and Angels. The seven faces, starting with the one nearest to the steps, represent:

1) **The Nativity and Visitation;** 2) **The Arrival and Adoration of the Magi;** 3) **The Presentation at the Temple; Joseph's Dream; the Flight into Egypt;** 4) **The Massacre of the Innocents;** 5) **The Crucifixion;** 6) **The Last Judgement of the Sinners;** 7) **The Last Judgement of the Good.**

The 8th square is covered by the steps that bear rich decorations and was re-designed by Riccio.

Let us continue our tour of the transept starting from the right.

The Chapel of St. Ansano – Near the altar we find a fresco by Francesco Vanni showing « **St. Ansano baptizing the Sienese »,** whilst on the left wall is a beautiful « **Monument to Cardinal Riccardo Petroni** », the work of Tino da Camaino (1317-18). The sarcophagus is upheld by four caryatids resting on corbels and is decorated with reliefs: on the front « **St. Thomas the disbeliever**, the **Resurrection,** the **Apparition of the Madonna »;** at the sides: « **Mary at the Sepulchre,** the **Meeting at Emmaus ».**

Above the sarcophagus is a tabernacle with pictures of the **Madonna and Child,** in the centre, with « **St. Peter »** and « **St. Paul »** at the sides.

The floor is covered with the tombstone of Bishop Giovanni Pecci, which was made out of bronze by Donatello in 1426.

Outside the Chapel we find:

– **the seated statue of Pius II**, by Giuseppe Mazzuoli (1968) and on the floor is a graffito tombstone dating from 1468.

The 1st altar: « **The Madonna with St. Peter and St. Paul »** which is a painting that was started by Salvatore Fontana and finished by Raffaele Vanni.

The 2nd altar: a 14th century wooden **Crucifix** with the statues of the **Virgin, John the Evangelist and Magdalen,** which date instead from the 17th century.

– The Statue of **Pius III** by Pietro Balestra (1706).

THE CHAPEL OF ST. JOHN THE BAPTIST has the same type of base as the Chapel of the Vow and is also arranged symmetrically, although its artistic content is quite

Saint Jean-Baptiste (Donatello - 1457)

different. It is, in fact, the work of Giovanni di Stefano who saw to its construction in the very evident Renaissance style. The white marble portal with bas-reliefs and inlaid work, was sculptured by Lorenzo Marrina, while the bases of the columns are attributed to Federighi and the wrought-iron gate is the work of Salustio Barili. The Chapel, which is richly decorated with stuccoes by Caponeri and Cosimo Lucchi (1596), treasures some important art works such as, starting from the left: the Portrait of **Alberto Aringhieri the Younger** by Pinturicchio (1504); the Statue of **St. Ansano** by Giovanni di Stefano (1487); the **Birth of John the Baptist** by Pinturicchio (1504); a bronze statue of **John the Baptist** by Donatello (1457); the **Beheading of John the Baptist** by Pinturicchio, re-done by Rustichino (1608); **St. Catherine of Alexandria,** statue by Neroccio and helpers (1487); the Portrait of **Alberto Aringhieri the Elder,** by Pinturicchio.

The upper area: **St. John the Baptist in the Desert** by Pinturicchio; the **Baptism of Jesus** by Rustici; the **Sermon of St. John** by Pinturicchio; **St. John in Prison** by Cesare Maccari.

The centre-piece of the Chapel is the **Baptismal Font,** which is the work of Antonio Federighi and which was made after 1484. It has an octagonal base and sculptured on the eight sides are the « **Six stories of Adam and Eve** », « **Samson and the Lion** », and « **Hercules and the Centaur** ».

The left nave – The first span encloses the **Piccolomini Library,** which was commissioned by Cardinal Francesco Piccolomini Todeschini – later elected Pope under the name of Pius III – starting from 1492 in order to house together the library belonging to his maternal uncle, Pontiff Pius II. The marble front presents two arches elegantly decorated by Marrina. The arch on the right has a small altar with bas-reliefs by Giovanni di Stefano that depict « **St. John the Baptist** » and a wooden group of the « **Pietà** » by Alberto di Betto; the left arch spans over the Library entrance and in the lunette above is a fresco by Pinturicchio, depicting the « **Crowning of Pope Pius III** ». The interior comprises a single, rectangular hall completely covered with frescoes by Pinturicchio, and it is really striking for the brightness and beauty of the colours. At the centre, supported by a Renaissance style stand, lies the group sculpture of the « **Three Graces** », which is a Roman copy dating from the 3rd century, of the original Greek sculpture of the Hellenic period. This art work was donated by Cardinal Francesco Piccolomini-Todeschini and destined to be placed in the Library.

The Library vault that was painted with frescoes by Pinturicchio in the years 1502-1503, is divided up into panels each bearing pictures of mythological and allegorical figures. At the centre, encircled by a garland of fruit, is the crest of the Piccolomini family. Arranged along the wall and bordered with pendentives and pilasters, are frescoes by the Umbrian master dating 1505-1508. They narrate the life of Enea Silvio Niccolomini, born in Corsignano (Pienza) in 1405, who was the Archishop of Siena, then Pontiff from 1458 to 1464.

The ten frescoes, considered most valuable for their dazzling chromatism and for their simple taste and liveliness of the narrative, are found starting from the window on the far right and they depict:

The Emperor Frederic III nominates him Poet Laureate (Pinturicchio)

1) the young Piccolomini departs for the Council of Basle;
2) he is the Council Ambassador at the court of King
James of Scotland; 3) the Emperor Frederick III nominates
him Poet Laureate; 4) he is sent by Frederick III as ambassador to Pope Eugenio IV; 5) the Bishop of Siena
presents Eleonora of Portugal to her fiancé Frederick III
at the Porta Camollia; 6) he is elected Cardinal by Pope
Callisto III; 7) he rises to the papal throne; 8) Pius II at
Mantua supports the Crusade against the Turks; 9) Pius II
proclaims the canonization of St. Catherine of Siena; 10)
Pius II travels to Ancona to hasten the start of the Crusade.
Underneath the frescoes one can find, placed on benches
inlaid by Antonio Barili (1496), some fabulous **choral books**
in illuminated manuscript by Liberale da Verona (1445-
1529) and by Girolamo da Cremona (early 15th century).
This work is a very fine and exquisite piece of craftsmanship that represents the highest expression of Italian
illuminated manuscript of the 15th century. Next to the
choral books of these two great masters, whose stay in
the Tuscan city was to leave its mark on Sienese painting
of the late 15th century, lie other valuable works of the
Sienese artists, namely Sano di Pietro, Pellegrino di Mariano and Guidoccio Cozzarelli.

The patterned majolica flooring of the hall represents the crests of the Piccolomini family. Lying above the entrance door is a bas-relief depicting **« Adam and Eve being expelled from the Garden of Eden »**, which is considered by some to be a copy of the original by Jacopo della Quercia for the Gaia Fountain, others, instead, attribute it to Jacopo della Quercia himself. Placed between the windows is a bronze statue of Christ risen again, sculptured by Fulvio Signorini (1595).

We now leave the Library and continue along the length of the nave:

- a sculptured monument representing **« Christ risen again and flanked by two Angels »**, by Bandino Bandini;
- the **Piccolomini Altar**, an exceptionally elegant work by Andrea Bregno (1503).

The niches surrounding the altar contain statues of **St. Gregory, St. Paul, St. Peter and St. Pius,** which are some of the early works of Michelangelo (1501-1504) who is said to have even finished the statue of St. Francis that was started by Torrigiani and which stands on the upper left hand side.

The 3rd altar - **« Epiphany »** by Pietro Sorri (1588);

the 2nd altar - **Christ with St. James and Philip,** by Franfesco Trevisani (1688);

the 1st altar - **Four Saints with Haloes,** again by Trevisani.

At the nave entrance stands the statue of **Pope Marcello II** by Domenico Cafaggi (1591).

Leaving the Duomo and continuing along the right flank we come to

THE NEW DUOMO

As mentioned earlier, in 1339 the Sienese planned a grand cathedral dedicated to the Virgin, which was to incorporate the already existing part of the Duomo. In fact, the latter became the Transept of the new and imposing longitudinal complex, which, according to plan, should have occupied the entire area of the present Square. The artists who supervised the construction work up until 1355, were Jacopo della Quercia, Lando di Pietro first, followed by Domenico di Agostino.

Today, the witnesses of this great project which, if realised, would have been one of the most imposing Gothic Cathedrals in Italy, remain apart from the two planimetrical layouts in parchment kept in the Trust Museum, the right nave with its cross-vaults, part of the left flank composed of three arches with huge windows, against which the Prefecture Residence was later constructed, and the immense wall of the facade, called **« the great face »**, entirely of marble with thin black stripes and lightened by very high, horizontally bipartite windows. These surviving parts, integrated by structural and decora-

tive elements completely or semi-finished, are quite sufficient to make us understand the great newness and exceptional historic importance of the colossal project.
The first three arches of the New Duomo's right nave house

THE METROPOLITAN TRUST MUSEUM

Constructed in 1870 and renovated quite a number of times afterwards, the Museum contains, most of all, those works of art created to embellish the Cathedral and subsequently transferred to the Museum not only to save them from deterioration, but also because in the course of the Cathedral's successive restorations in the 16th and 17th centuries, the original art works were substituted by other works.

The collection comprises sculptural and pictorial groups, objects in bronze, wood and terra cotta, gold crafts, embroidery and illuminated manuscripts, all works of an immense artistic value. Naturally, there are also the famous masterpieces of Sienese and Tuscan art of the period from the 13th to the 15th century, making this Museum one of the richest and most important in the whole of Italy.

THE GROUND FLOOR – We enter a large hall that is divided into two rooms by a great wrought-iron gate of the 15th century, which rests on richly sculptured marble plutei of the Nicola Pisano school.

THE FIRST ROOM – Near the left wall we can view the following:
– a **high-relief,** perhaps of the late 13th century, originating from Pieve di Ponte allo Spino, in the vicinity of Sovicille, which depicts the **Annunciation, Nativity, Flight into Egypt and Epiphany;** – the front of a **Roman sarcophagus,** belonging to the Imperial period, which is decorated with figures of sea gods; – a marble pluteus with the **Mater Ecclesiae and symbols of the Evangelists,** attributed to Lapo of the Giovanni Pisano school; – **St. Bernardine:** a bas-relief by Urbano da Cortona; – **St. Peter:** a statue also by Urbano da Cortona; – a lion by Giovanni Pisano.

THE SECOND ROOM – Situated immediately behind the gate are the two She-Wolves that originally belonged to the columns in front of the facade of the Duomo. The one on the right is said to be by Giovanni Pisano, while the left one is by Urbano da Cortona.

At the centre of this huge hall we find a splendid high-relief that demonstrates the extreme maturity of Jacopo della Quercia, and represents the « **Madonna and Child, St. Jerome and Cardinal Antonio Casini genuflecting before them** ». This work was originally placed on the altar of Cardinal Casini, but for a long period of time it disappeared and only returned to the scene a few years ago.

Madonna and Child, St. Jerome and Cardinal Antonio Casini genuflecting before them

Mary of Moses - Abacuc (Giovanni Pisano)

On the floor we find a tombstone of Tommaso Pecci (14th century) and the original fragments of the Cathedral's flooring, four of which depict biblical stories by Becca-fumi and six the Ages of Man by Antonio Federighi.

Leaning against the pillars are TEN STATUES that were sculptured by Giovanni Pisano for the Duomo's facade and, which were transferred to the Museum starting from the latter half of the last century. These statues were made during the period 1285 and 1296 and represent biblical characters, ancient philosophers and prophets. They are of much larger size than the normal statues and are considered a masterpiece of Giovanni Pisano's crafts-manship, as well as being one of the most important and oldest complexes of European Gothic sculpture. Let us begin from the left:

– **Moses, Mary of Moses, Simon, a Sibyl, Isaiah, Balaam, David, Abacuc, Plato and Solomon.**

Lying between one pillar and the next are 14th century statues of the Pisano school, and it is reputed that Pisano himself directly collaborated in the sculpture of certain of them.

Along the left wall are:

– the **Madonna and Child and Christ's** forefathers, frag-ments of the facade rose-window of the Duomo by Gio-vanni di Cecco.

– **Two bulls and a horse** by Giovanni Pisano.

The end wall is decorated with a great altar-piece, by

The grand Majesty by Duccio di Buoninsegna

Brescianino and his helpers (1524), placed on a Baroque altar and representing the « **Baptism of Christ** ».

THE FIRST FLOOR – THE DUCCIO HALL – It is so named because of the grand MAJESTY altarpiece, which is the masterpiece of **Duccio di Buoninsegna** (1278-1318), considered Siena's first great artist who knew how to extract poetical themes from the most diverse suggestions, harmonizing the precious pomp of the Byzantine framework with the human lyricism of French Gothic. The monumental painting, commissioned on the 9th October, 1308, and finished by the artist in about three years, that was later praised highly and celebrated by chroniclers of the era, was destined to adorn the main altar of the Duomo, where it was installed on the 9th June, 1311. Two centuries later, the painting was removed and after having been separated into two parts, it was transferred to the Trust Museum in 1878.

Originally, this work was composed of a huge central canvas representing the « **Madonna seated on a throne and holding Baby Jesus,** amidst two worshipping groups of **Angels and Saints** ». In this painting we can clearly see how the cultural components of the art of Duccio perfectly merge and harmonize together.

On one side, there is Duccio's Byzantine tendency, displayed in the general arrangement of the group in a frontal position with the gold background of the panel. On the other, great refinement and the presence of Gothic linear elements, visible in the cusp above the Madonna and in the rich, but not overdone draping of Mary's mantle. However, the general orchestration of the painting overcomes the particularity of Duccio's artistic components: the solemnity and preciousness of the whole is redeemed by the slow, sweet movements of the heads of the Angels and Saints, whilst a serene and intimate note of lyricism gives a human touch to the faces and gestures.

Illustrated in 26 panels on the rear of the altar-piece, placed in front of the Majesty, are **Stories of Christ's Passion** that are separated by a wide, middle band marking an interval between the initial scenes, in lower order, and the last scenes in the higher order.

The altar-piece was also decorated with a predella, which displays on the front, **Seven stories of Christ's Childhood,** and on the rear, 10 panels on Public Life, as well as a Gothic fastigium comprising of 16 panels. The front depicts the life of the Madonna and the rear that of Christ risen again. Out of these latter panels, five have been lost forever, some are in museums and in collections abroad and only 19 panels are kept in this museum, together with the front and rear of the art work.

Here is a reading of the 26 rear panels, starting from the upper left:

1/2 - **Christ sent to Pilate and Christ before Herod;**

The Crucifixion (Duccio di Buoninsegna)

3/4 - **the Flagellation and the Crowning with thorns;**
5/6 - **the Walk to Calvary and Pilate who washes his
hands;** 7 - **the Crucifixion;** 8/9 - **the Deposition in the
Sepulchre and Deposition from the Cross;** 10/11 - **Mary at
the Sepulchre and the Descent to Limbo;** 12/13 - **the
Apparition of Emmaus and « Noli me tangere ».**
The Panels below:
14 - **Entrance to Jerusalem;** 15/16 - **the Washing of feet
and the Last Supper;** 17/18 - **Judas's Pact and Christ's
dismissal;** 19/20 - **Judas's Kiss and Praying in the Olive
Grove;** 21/22 - **Christ before Ann and the Denial by Peter;**

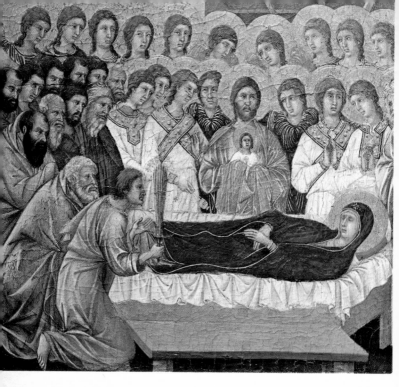

Death of Mary (Duccio di Buoninsegna)

23/24 - Christ beaten and Christ before Caifa; 25/26 - Christ accused by the Pharisees and Christ before Pilate. In the same hall we also find, on the right wall, the **« Birth of the Virgin »,** a masterpiece by Pietro Lorenzetti that is signed and dated 1342, as well as the **« Madonna and Child »,** which is an early work of Duccio, originating from the Church of St. Cecilia at Crevanile in the vicinity of Murlo. From the Duccio Hall we cross, through a door on the right, into a room containing 16th century animals designed by Riccio, and then into another hall where eight codices of the 14th and 15th century are kept, together with numerous documents relating to architectural designs and projects of artists who worked on the Duomo's construction.

A door on the left in the Duccio Hall gives access to another hall displaying 19th century cartoons on the Cathedral flooring.

THE TREASURY ROOM — This room can been found halfway between the first and second floors and, apart from the art works, it also safeguards the most precious sacred vestments and vessels of the Duomo. Here is a

The Madonna with Large Eyes

list of some of them:
– **Reliquary of the head of St. Galgano,** a 13th century work of great craftsmanship, originating from the St. Galgano Abbey; – **Reliquary of St. Clement** (17th century); – **Silk frontal embroidered in gold and silver** (16th century); – **St. John the Evangelist,** statue by Giacomo Cozzarelli; – **St. Galgano's Crown,** of the late 13th century; – **Golden Rose,** donated by Alexander VII in 1658; – **St. Jerome,** a sketch by Bernini; – Small wooden **Crucifix** by Giovanni Pisano, which is flanked by figures of the Madonna and St. John the Evangelist both by Giovanni di Paolo; – Polychrome wooden busts of the **Saints Crescenzio, Vittore and Savino,** three masterpieces by Francesco di Valdambrino (1409); – **Lament on the death of Christ,** a detached fresco by Vecchietta; – **Christ carrying the cross** by Beccafumi, bordered by an inlaid frame by Antonio Barili; – **Madonna and Child,** attributed to Benvenuto di Giovanni.

THE SECOND FLOOR – We enter, straightaway, into the HALL OF THE MADONNA WITH THE LARGE EYES.
In the centre of the hall, we find a Madonna and Child,

also known as the **Madonna with the Large Eyes,** belonging to the early 13th century.

This represents one of the oldest Sienese paintings and originally, its place was over the main altar of the Duomo, much before Duccio's Majesty was installed. Just prior to the Battle of Montaperti, the people of Siena knelt down in prayer before this very painting.

On the walls, from left to right, we have:

– **Four Saints:** parts of a polyptych by Ambrogio Lorenzetti; – **Articles of the Creed:** nine panels attributed to Nicola di Naldo; – **St. Jerome** by Giovanni di Paolo; – **The Blessed Agostino Novello** inspired by an Angel and Four of His Miracles: a masterpiece by Simone Martini, transferred here temporarily from the St. Agostino Church; – **Cabinet doors** painted by Benedetto di Bindo and helpers (1411-12); – **Madonna and Child,** attributed to Sassetta; – **Apparition of St. Francis in the Chapter of Asles,** by Giovanni di Paolo; – **Madonna and Saints,** polyptych by Gregorio di Cecco; – **Crucifixion** dating from the early 15th century; – **Madonna and Child,** by Matteo di Giovanni, originating from the Church of Percenna in the vicinity of Buonconvento; – **Madonna and Child, Angels and the Saints Apollonia and Bernardino,** by Sano di Pietro; – **Madonna and Child,** by one of Duccio's followers reputedly named the Master of the City of Castello.

THE CONVERSATION ROOM – Here, in 1777, Vittorio Alfieri wrote some of his tragedies. Amongst the works kept here are:

– **St. Anthony of Padua,** attributed to Matteo Balducci; – **Madonna enthroned and amidst the Saints John the Evangelist,** Nicholas, Gregory and Jerome, with a predella by Giovanni (1479); – **Madonna** enthroned and admist the Saints Anthony of Padua, and Bernardino, signed by Matteo di Giovanni and dated 1460.

Apart from this hall, there is another room adorned with mural hangings originating from the ex-monastery of CAMPANSI.

From here, we can climb the spiral staircase up to the top of the « great face », from where we will be able to admire at close quarters the bell-tower and dome of the Duomo.

Once back under the arches of the New Duomo, by way of the door opening out at the back, and then down the Sabatelli stairway, we arrive in Piazza San Giovanni, the site of the Baptistry.

THE BAPTISTRY

The Baptistry, or Pieve di San Giovanni, forms the base of the extension to the Duomo's head-piece in the guise of a crypt. The facade, which was begun in 1317 and resumed in 1382, and which was wrongly attributed to Giacomo di Mino del Pelliciaio, is perhaps the work of

The Baptistry

Domenico di Agostino.
Three great portals open out the lower part and a cusp surmounts the central one. Above these portals, separated by groups of small columns and marble decorations, lies an extremely delicate crown of hanging arches. Three tall ogival windows give a finishing touch to the upper area. In front of the portals the flooring, which is quite damaged, displays marble graffiti depicting Sacraments of Baptism and Confirmation. The one in front of the left door represents the « **Birth of man to the material life** » and it is the work of Bartolomeo di Mariano (1450); the other two depict **Baptism** scenes in front of the central door, and **Confirmation** scenes in front of the right door, both carried out by Federighi in 1451.

The Baptistry interior is wide and bright and the construction was finished in 1325 under the able supervision of Camaino da Crescentino and Tino da Camaino. It is rectangular in shape and is divided into three naves; the whole upper part is covered with frescoes by Vecchietta and his school.

– vaults near the facade: **Apostles** by Vecchietta; – under the arches: figures of **Sibyls and Prophets** by Vecchietta; – other vaults: **Articles of the Creed,** by the Vecchietta school (1450); – right lunette: **Jesus in the house of the Pharisees,** by Pietro di Francesco degli Orioli (1489); – upper part of the Apse: **the life of Jesus,** by Michele di Matteo of Bologna (1447); – lower part of the Apse: the **life of Jesus,** by the Vecchietta school; – left lunette: **St. Anthony's Miracles,** by Benvenuto di Giovanni.

Near the entrance, there is a holy-water stoup made by Federighi (1482); a niche on the left wall contains a wooden statue of St. John the Baptist, by the Jacopo della Quercia school.

Capture of the Baptist (Lorenzo Ghiberti) and the Angel annonces the birth of the Baptist tho Zaccaria (Jacopo della Quercia)

Herod's Banquet (Donatello - 1427)

Lying in the middle and slightly raised on two steps, is the Baptistry's most valuable art work, **The Baptismal Font,** which is considered one of the greatest masterpieces of 15th century sculpture, where Gothic elegance is accompanied by and merges with the harmony of Renaissance.

The Font is made up of an hexagonal basin with a pillar above it supporting an hexagonal ciborium. The architectural part was carried out in the period 1428-30, by Pietro del Minella, Bastiano di Corso and Nanni di Lucca, while the sculptures are by different artists. However, in spite of this variety, the font possesses an admirable stylistic unity and can be considered a true masterpiece of statuary and sculptural art.

Baptism of Christ (Lorenzo Ghiberti - 1427)

The ciborium designed by Jacopo della Quercia, is topped by a beautiful statue of **St. John the Baptist** by the same Jacopo and, adorning the part between the pediments of the sides are **four bronze angels:** two by Donatello and two by Giovanni di Turino (1424). The niches contain the figures of five prophets by Jacopo della Quercia and a Madonna and Child by Giovanni di Turino.

The basin, which is wrongly attributed to Jacopo della Quercia, presents six bas-reliefs in gilded bronze, depicting the **Life of St. John the Baptist;** six statues separate each bas-relief.

Starting from the panel placed in front of the altar and continuing towards the right hand side, we have:

Statue of Hope and of Faith by Donatello

– **Zacchariah expelled from the temple,** by Jacopo della Quercia (1417); – **Statue of Justice,** by Giovanni di Turino (1424); – **Birth of St. John the Baptist,** by Turino di Sano (1427); – **Statue of Charity,** by Giovanni di Turino (1424); – **St. John the Baptist's preachings,** by Giovanni di Turino (1427); – **Statue of Prudence,** by Giovanni di Turino; – **Baptism of Christ,** by Lorenzo Ghiberti (1427); – **Statue of Faith,** by Donatello; – **Capture of St. John the Baptist,** by Lorenzo Ghiberti (1427); – **Statue of Hope,** by Donatello (1428); – **Herod's Banquet,** by Donatello (1427); – **Statue of Fortitude**, by Goro di Neroccio (1428).

We return to the Piazza del Duomo by climbing up the steep steps and, facing the Cathedral facade, on its right we can admire the **Ducal Palace,** which today is the seat of the Prefecture. Its construction was begun in 1489 by Giacomo Petrucci and extended towards the end of the year 1600, following Bernardo Buontalenti's project and by order of the Medici family, who were governing at that time.

The **Archibishops Palace** stands on the left and appears almost to unite itself with the Duomo. It was erected in 1718-23 in the 14th century Gothic style, copied from the Cathedral in order to match the two buildings: the lower part of the facade has white and black stripes while the upper part is of plain brickwork. The interior houses the extremely interesting « **Chapel of St. Biagio** », which is the work of Riccio, and a gilded shrine containing the « **Madonna of Milk** », Ambrogio Lorenzetti's masterpiece done on a cusped panel, which takes one's breath away for its bright colours and the moving scene.

Instead, in front of the Cathedral stands the Santa Maria della Scala Hospital, which takes its name from the fact that it is situated facing the Duomo stairway. According to tradition, it was founded in about 832 by Beato Sorore, a Sienese shoemaker, and the present building was constructed thanks to the Canons of the Duomo. The external architecture partly preserves the features of a construction belonging to the late 1200 and early 1300. The facade is done partly in ashlar and partly in brickwork and is spanned by large mullioned windows. The interior treasures numerous frescoes that prove interesting, even though they are rather damaged, in order to better understand the costumes and architecture of that period.

Certain paintings are dedicated to exalting the care of the sick and hospital work.

On entering we find the first Vestibule that holds the tomb of Jacopo Tondi, very likely the work of Giacomo Cozzarelli. The beautiful Renaissance ceiling was done in around 1460 by Guidoccio d'Andrea. We then pass into the second Vestibule, where we can view a fresco by Beccafumi; in the adjoining room are half-figures of Saints, attributed to

Cristoforo di Bindoccio and Meo di Pietro, Lorenzetti's followers.

In the Infirmary Hall, that dedicated to St. Galgano, we find a Crucifixion by Martino di Bartolomeo.

The **Church of Santa Maria della Scala** or DELLA SANTISSIMA ANNUNZIATA, can be reached either by way of the door near the Hospital entrance, or by crossing the first vestibule of the Hospital. The church was erected in 1252 and renovated by Guidoccio d'Andrea in 1465, and has a single nave with a raised presbytery, a wide apse and a thick lacunar ceiling. Also of great interest are the two wonderful organs inlaid by Ventura di Ser Giuliano Turapilli, to whom we must also attribute the elegant wooden choir of the apse, as well as the beautiful bronze statue of Christ risen again, by Vecchietta (1476), and the bright fresco by Sebastiano Conca (1732) that covers the choir and depicts the large basin outside the Temple of Jerusalem in which the sacrificial beasts were cleansed. The Sacristy Treasury is of great value and comprises rich goldsmiths art dating from the 10th to the 16th century and pottery of the 14th to the 16th century.

From the first vestibule of the hospital we can visit the CHAPEL OF THE SICK, which is adorned with paintings by Giuseppe Nasini depicting stories of the Life of Mary. The altar bears a **Madonna** by Paolo di Giovanni Fei.

Underneath the hospital vaults, adjacent to the Oratory of St. Catherine of the Night, where the Saint slept in a cell after having assisted the sick of the « Pilgrimage », lies the **Brotherhood of the Flagellants**, which was once a catacomb known as the Consecrated Grave of the Flagellants, and now belongs to the Society of the Executors of Pious Orders.

This Brotherhood possesses a « **Madonna and the Saints Peter and Paul** » by Alessandro Casolani, adorning the main altar, a **Crucifix** and two wooden statues of the 16th century depicting St. Bernardine and St. Catherine.

In the Sacristy we find a « **Last Judgement** » attributed to Martino di Bartolomeo, « **St. John the Baptist** », by Giovanni di Paolo, and a « **Pietà** » by Sano di Pietro.

The streets Via dei Fusari and Vicolo San Girolamo, on the left of the Bishops Palace, descend into the picturesque little square where stands the **Church of St. Sebastian in Valle Piatta,** or Rotunda of the Innocents, of the Wood District.

Near the main altar lies a **Madonna** of the 15th century; at the sides of the Presbytery are a **Madonna and Saints** perhaps of the 16th century and another **Madonna and Saints** by Benvenuto di Giovanni; hanging near the right altar is a **Crucifixion** by Rutilio Manetti. Also treasured here are a precious reliquary of the second half of the 14th century and some Palio trophies won by the District.

ITINERARY 3

National Art Gallery (Palazzo Buonsignori) - **House of Pia Tolomei** - **Church of St. Peter at the Steps** - **The Palazzo Pollini** - **Church of San Niccolò al Carmine** - **Chapel of the Prisons of St. Ansano** - **Church of St. Augustine** - **The Arch of St. Joseph.**

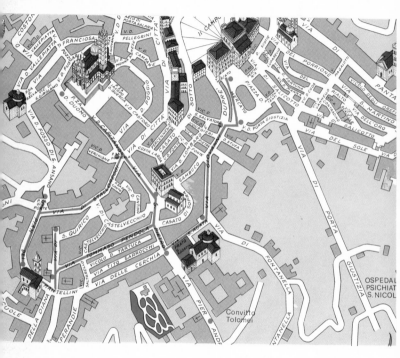

We return to the Duomo Square and then walk, once again, through Via del Capitano, past **Piazza Postierla,** commonly known as PIAZZA OF THE FOUR CORNERS because it is situated at the crossing of five streets, until we arrive in Via San Pietro where we find, standing at number 29, the BUONSIGNORI RESIDENCE. This is one of the most elegant late-Gothic buildings of the city, constructed after 1440 by the rich Sienese banker, Giovanni di Guccio Bichi, who a few years later, sold it to the Tegliacci brothers. In 1476, it became the property of the Buonsignori family, the last descendent of which donated the building to the city so that it be turned into a Museum. The facade is made of brick with a stone basement and it represents one of the last examples of Gothic architecture. The lower portion presents blind arches, while the first and second floors have elegant three-mullioned windows divided by

84

a cornice of small hanging arches. The merlons of the crown contain marble panels bearing stucco heads.

NATIONAL ART GALLERY

Today, this residence is the seat of the NATIONAL ART GALLERY, which boasts a collection of art-works of fundamental importance for a perfect understanding of Sienese painting, that date from the end of the 12th to the first half of the 17th century. The Gallery's origin dates from the end of the 18th century, when Abbott Giuseppe Ciaccheri collected together a number of paintings as a donation to the city of Siena. Following this, works received as donations from deposits, churches, convents, religious or suppressed lay brotherhoods, all helped to enrich this collection even further. The collection was first kept in the Institute of Fine Arts, then in 1930, it was transferred permanently to the Buonsignori Residence, governed by the State. The art gallery possesses about 700 paintings arranged in 38 halls either in chronological order, or in order of style.

Works of great masters and less famous artists are all present here; works constituting authentic masterpieces

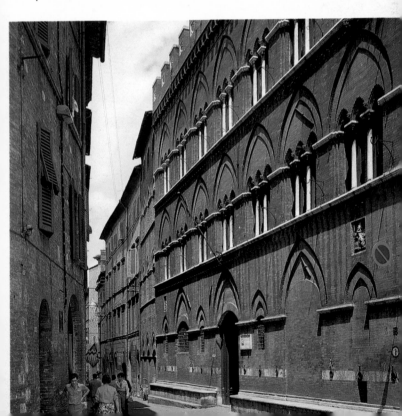

known the world over are displayed at the side of less important ones, but they all contribute towards creating a patrimony of priceless art-works, as well as forming the most unique evidence of Siena's school of painting, which was, in the words of Roberto Paribeni « a perfect impresison of an entire world, a gentle, fluorishing synthesis of Italy's great spiritual riches ».

In the entrance hall we find a high-relief depicting Victory and a sarcophagus, both belonging to the Roman period. We then pass into the elegant Courtyard along whose walls are displayed various sculptures of the 14th century and coats-of-arms. On the left wall we can admire the **« Life of the Blessed Gioacchino Piccolomini »** and **« Annunciation »**, **« Noli me tangere »**, **« Jesus on the road to Emmans »**, all bas-reliefs of the 14th century; **« Four statues of the Evangelists »**; **« St. Paul »**; **« Moses »**; statues attributed to Giovanni di Turino.

Turning right, we enter into the Hall of Cartoons, where we find displayed nine huge cartoons of biblical scenes, done by Beccafumi for the flooring of the Duomo. Also, there are bronze bracelets by Giacomo Cozzarelli, a fragmentary fresco by Guidoccio Cozzarelli, a large canvas by Pietro da Cortona and a sketch by Vecchietta for the bronze ciborium of the Duomo's main altar. We shall now begin a thorough tour of the art gallery and the entrance hall; and to do this we must go straight up to the second floor because the works are arranged in chronological order. We will point out here those works considered most important.

Hall 1. (1) - **Frontal with the Redeemer and symbols of the Evangelists,** and at the sides, in six sections, three **stories of the Cross** and three of a Saint, identified by some as being St. Helen. This is the first work of Sienese painting that bears a definite date (1215). (8) - **Transfiguration, Christ entering Jerusalem, Resurrection of Lazarus,** a frontal by Guido da Siena, which is a very rare medieval painting on canvas.

Hall 2. (15) - **St. Peter enthroned, with sacred stories at the sides,** a frontal attributed either to Guido da Siena or his school. (9-13) - **Stories of Christ** by Guido da Siena. They are perhaps the Majesty panels belonging to the Palazzo Pubblico. (14) - **St. John the Baptist enthroned,** and at the sides are twelve stories of his life, work of the Sienese school, carried out between the years 1270 and 1280.

Hall 3. (47) - **Madonna and Child and the Saints Agnes, John the Evangelist, John the Baptist and Magdalen,** all by Duccio di Buoninsegna and his helpers. **Madonna of the Misericordia,** by Niccolò di Segna. (28) - **Madonna and Child and the Saints Augustine, Paul, Peter and Domenico,** by Duccio di Buoninsegna. Works by Ugolino di Nerio and the Duccio school.

Madonna of the Franciscans (Duccio di Buoninsegna)

Hall 4. (20) - **Madonna of the Franciscans,** probably dating around 1300. It is one of the most beautiful works carried out by Duccio, whose art, which is founded on the most ancient of Byzantine traditions, reaches an extremely refined and pathetically human tone. Works by Ugolino di Nerio, Maestro of Città di Castello, Maestro of Badia a Isola, Segna di Bonaventura.

Hall 5. (104) - **Adoration of the Magi,** probably the master-piece of Bartolo di Fredi, done in the period 1370-80. This work is highly praised for its rich detail and the lively colours. Other works by Bartolo di Fredi and a beautiful polyptych by Nicolò Tegliacci and Luca di Tommè.

Hall 6. Madonna and Child, one of Simone Martini's best

Adoration of the Magi (Bartolo di Fredi)

and perfect creations. (595) - **Madonna and Child** by Lippo Memmi.

Hall 7. (77) - Madonna and Child and the Saints Mary Magdalen and Doroty, a polyptych by Ambrogio Lorenzetti dating around 1332. (70-71) - **City by the sea and Castle on the lake shore.** These two panels by Ambrogio Lorenzetti belong to the Town Archives and are among the most valuable works of the Gallery's collection. But their value does not mean their artistic content only: they are, in fact, the first paintings out of all European art, to have purely landscapes as their subjects. **Madonna and Child** by Ambrogio Lorenzetti. (65) - **Madonna and**

Child, Saints, Doctors of the Church and Angels, by Ambrogio Lorenzetti. These are sublime works for their harmony of colours and gentle, flowing lines. (88) - Annunciation, another of Ambrogio Lorenzetti's masterpieces, signed and dated 1344. This is the artist's last work known to us. (83-84) - Stories of the Carmelite Order. (62-64) - St. Thaddeus and St. Bartholomew, St. Thomas and Jacob. These latter three paintings form the central part, the predella and the sides of the great altarpiece painted by Pietro Lorenzetti in 1328-29, for the Church of Carmine. The artful statuary plasticity, the severe harmony of a few dominant colours and a dynamic tension of the lines, display in this masterpiece the maturity of the artist. (116) - Birth of the Virgin with Saints Jacob, Catherine of Alexandria, Bartholomew and Elizabeth of Hungary, by Paolo di Giovanni Fei.

The following can be found in this hall, together with other works by Lorenzetti and his followers.
(61) - Assumption of the Virgin, by the Maestro of San Pietro Ovile (about 1360). (300) - Madonna and Child, three Saints and Daniel the Prophet, a unique work signed by Paolo di Giovanni Fei. (145) - Polyptych by Giacomo di Mino del Pellicciaio, dating 1362. Wooden statue of St. John the Baptist, by Domenico di Niccolò of the Choirs.

Annunciation (A. Lorenzetti - 1344)

City by the sea (A. Lorenzetti)

Hall 8. (92) - **Allegory of Sin and Redemption,** attributed to Pietro Lorenzetti. (50) - **Madonna and Child and Four Saints**, attributed to Pietro Lorenzetti. (114) - **Crucifix with two Prophets,** triptych by Andrea Vanni. (592) - **Madonna and Child,** by the Master of the Majesty of London. (18) - **Madonna and Child,** by the Duccio School.

Hall 9. (164) - **Madonna and Child and Angels** by Domenico di Bartolo dating 1433. (171) - **Wedding of St. Catherine of Alexandria, St. John the Baptist and St. Anthony the Abbot,** by Michelino da Besozzo. It is the sole work signed by this artist, who is so important for the birth of international painting in Lombardy. (607) - **Crucifixion,** by Niccolò di Pietro Gerini. (60) - **Madonna and Child,**

Saints and Angels, by Bernardo Daddi (1336). (110) - **The Four Evangelists,** attributed to Antonio Veneziano. (157) - **Triptych** by Lorenzo Monaco.

Hall 10. (137) - **Wedding of St. Catherine of Alexandria** and three Saints, by Paolo di Giovanni Fei. (146) - **Madonna and Child**, two Saints and a Crucifixion, all by the same artist.

In the tiny 18th century chapel stands a small coloured statue of the Madonna, which is attributed to Giacomo Cozzarelli.

Hall 11. Here we find some works by Taddeo di Bartolo. (132) - **Adoration of the Shepherds. Annunciation and Saints.** (128) - **Madonna and Child and Saints.** (127) - **Adoration of the Magi.** (160) - **Madonna and Child** and Four Saints, a polyptych by Martino di Bartolomeo. (219) - **Madonna and Child** and the Saints Philip and Jacob, by Andrea di Bartolo.

Hall 12. This hall displays a collection of works by Giovanni di Paolo. (212) - **Christ forbearing and Christ triumphant.** (174-175-176) - **Presentation of Mary at the Temple,** Crucifixion and Flight into Egypt. (200) - **Crucifixion** signed and dated 1440. (190-201) - **St. Mary Magdalen, St. Galgano, St. Bernardo, St. Romualdo,** sides of a polyptych.

The Flight into Egypt (Giovanni di Paolo)

Hall 13. (172) - **Last Judgement with Heaven and Hell,** one of Giovanni di Paolo's best works. (167) - **Last Supper,** by Sassetta.

This is the artist's very first work and it is of great importance in the history of 15th century Sienese painting. The work recalls the styles of Simone Martini and Pietro Lorenzetti, but has an entirely new approach. (166) - **St. Anthony the Abbot** thrashed by the Devils, again by Sassetta. (206) - **Madonna of Meekness**, by Giovanni di Paolo, about 1445. (177) - **Madonna and Child** and the Saints Catherine of Alexandria and John the Baptist. This is a small triptych by the Maestro dell'Osservanza. Here, we also find those other parts which, together with the Last Supper, form the altar-piece painted by Sassetta expressly for the Wool Guild.

Madonna and Child (Neroccio di Bartolomeo Landi)

Hall 14. Neroccio di Bartolomeo's works.

(281) - **Madonna and Child and the Saints Jerome and Bernardino.** (282) - **Madonna and Child** between the Saints Michael and Bernardino. (295) - **Madonna and Child, Magdalen and St. John the Baptist.** (294) - Madonna and Child and the Saints John the Baptist and Andrew, all bordered by a 15th century frame. (285) - Madonna and Child and the Saints Bernardino and Catherine of Siena.

Matteo di Giovanni's works.

(286) - **Madonna and Child and Angels.** (283) - **Madonna and Child.** (400) - **Madonna and Child and the Saints Michael and Magdalen.** (280) - **Madonna and Child** and the Saints John the Evangelist and Jacob. (399) - **Madonna and Child** and the Saints John the Evangelist and Francis.

Francesco di Giorgio Martini's works.

(277) - **Annunciation.** (437) - **Nativity with** St. Bernardino and St. Tommaso d'Aquino. (288) - **Madonna and Child and an Angel.** (293) - **Madonna and Child and the Saints Jacob and Jerome.** (274-276) - **Joseph and the wife of Putifar,** Susanna bathing, the selling of Joseph, all panels of a Nuptial Chest.

Hall 15.

(279) - **Adoration of the Shepherds** with the Saints Galgano and Martino, the only work signed by Pietro di Domenico. (365) - **Adoration of the Shepherds** with various Saints, by Andrea di Niccolò. (217) - **Triumph of David,** the front of a chest by Neroccio.

Hall 16. Works by Sano di Pietro.

(237) - **Madonna and Child and the Saints Margaret,** Catherine of Alexandria, Bernardino and Frances. (224) - **Madonna and Child** surrounded by eight Angels. (265) - **St. Jerome in the desert.** In this hall we also find works by the Maestro dell'Osservanza. (218) - **Pietà with the Capture and Martyrdom** of St. Bartholomew, a predella belonging to a triptych. (216) - **Crucifixion, St. Ambrose humiliates Theodosius,** St. Jerome in the desert, all belonging to this same triptych.

Hall 17. Works by Sano di Pietro.

(269) - **Coronation of the Virgin and Four Saints.** (233) - **Madonna and Child,** St. Jerome, the Blessed Giovanni Colombini and the Saints Cosma and Damiano and in the cusps, St. Peter (249) and **the Annunciation.**

Hall 18. Also this hall contains Sano di Pietro's works.

(241) - **The Madonna entrusts Siena to Pope Callisto II.** (246) - **Madonna and Child,** the Blessed Giovanni Colombini and Four Saints. This work dated 1444, is considered one of the best works of Sano di Pietro.

Hall 19.

(440) - **Coronation of the Virgin,** by Francesco di Giorgio Martini. (431) - **Madonna and Child and the Saints Sebastiano,** Girolamo Antonio and Nicola, by Bernardino Fungai (1512). (434) - **Ascension.** by Benvenuto di Giovanni (1491).

The Madonna entrusts Siena to Pope Callisto II (Sano di Pietro)

(205) - **St. Bernardino** and, underneath, Sermon of St. Bernardine, by Vecchietta. (210) - **Madonna and Child and the Saints** Peter, Paul, Lorenzo and Francesco, a huge plate by Vecchietta.
From the second floor we can go up to the third, where the Spannocchi collection has been arranged, together with other works that were once displayed in different halls of the Gallery. Here, we can admire a number of important works by Dutch and German Masters, such as Albrecht Dürer and Christopf Amberger, as well as those of Italian Masters, namely Lotto, Moroni and Padovanino.

Hall 20.
(298) - **Madonna and Child and the Saints Catherine of Alexandria,** Agostino, Sebastiano and Monica, by Andrea di Niccolò (1500). (309) - **Annunciation,** by Girolamo da Cremona. (388) - **Madonna and Child and two Saints,** by Pacchiarotti. (581) - **« Noli me tangere »,** by Benvenuto di Giovanni, dating from around 1510.

Hall 21. This hall is closed because it is in the course of preparation.

Hall 22. Madonna and Child and Four Saints and a predella with four panels. This polyptych dates 1430 and is by Bicci di Lorenzo. (346) **Angel,** by Matteo Balducci. (383) - **Assumption of the Virgin**, perhaps by Cosimo Rosselli.

Hall 23. Works by Matteo Balducci.

(422) - **Ascension** by Pacchiarotti. (426) - **Visitation and two Saints**, again by Pacchiarotti. (441) - **Assumption of the Virgin and Saints,** by Fungai. (495) - **The Holy Family** with St. John, an elegant and exquisite tondo by Pinturicchio.

Hall 24. **Madonna and Child,** by Rutilio Manetti. **St. George seated between two Virtues,** by Ventura Salimbeni. (633) - **Deposition** by Giuseppe Bazzani. Mora Players by Antiveduto Grammatica.

The Holy Family (Pinturicchio)

Hall 25. (625) - **Martyrdom** by Rutilio Manetti, dating 1613. (626) - **St. Eligio and the plague-stricken,** a masterpiece by Manetti, who can be considered the most important Sienese painter of the 17th century.

HALL 26 — (61) - **The Vestal Tuccia demonstrates her innocence,** a huge canvas by Rutilio Manetti.

HALL 27 — (457) - **The Holy Family and two Saints** by **Innocenzo** da Imola. (563) - **Madonna and Child and St. John,** of the Andrea del Sarto school. **Resurrection** by Giorgio Vasari (1550).

HALL 28 — In this small hall we find three panels by Andrea del Brescianino done in the early period of the artist's career. (650) - **Charity.** (651) - **Hope.** (652) - **Fortitude.**

Lucretia (School of Luca Cranach - XIV century)

HALL 29 – (403) - **Paradise by Riccio**. (419) - **Annunciation and Visitation** by Girolamo del Pacchia (1518). (574) - **The Holy Family with Catherine of Siena,** probably by Beccafumi. (444-447) - **Coronation of the Virgin** and predella by Riccio.

HALL 30 – This hall is dedicated to Sodoma and Beccafumi, the most famous Sienese painters of the first half of the 16th century. Here are some of their works: (357) - **St. Catherine of Siena.** (512) - **Nativity** dated 1503, an early work of great beauty. Works by Beccafumi: (384) - **Trinity and four Saints dated 1513.** (438) - **Madonna and Child** and Saints Paul and Galgano.

HALL 31 – (369) - **Lament at the death of Christ,** by Giromo di Benvenuto. (352) - Christ at the pillar, by Sodoma.

Jesus at the Column (Sodoma)

Queen Elizabeth of England (Federico Zuccari)

A work of great spiritual nobility and stylistic refinement, which formed part of an even larger work carried out during the period 1511 and 1.514 for the Convent of St. Francesco in Siena.

HALL 32 – This hall also contains works by Sodoma. Of particular interest is the renowned panel entitled **« Deposition from the Cross »** (1413).

HALL 33 – Works by Beccafumi: (344) - **Baptism of Christ.** (420) - **St. Catherine** receives the stigmata (about 1515), one the artist's masterpieces. The predella of the panel relates three stories of the life of St. Catherine. (601) - **Self-Portrait** by Francesco Vanni. (408) - Predella by Andrea del Brescianino.

HALLS 34 – 36 are presently in the course of preparation. **HALL 37** – (427) - **Christ's descent into Limbo**, a fantastic work by Beccafumi (1530-35). (443-401) - **Christ's descent into Limbo** and the Sermon in the Garden of Gethsemene, other masterpieces by Sodoma, that date around 1525.

A little beyond Palazzo Buonsignori, in Via San Pietro, stands the **HOUSE OF PIA TOLOMEI**, which is an elegant and ancient residence of the Pannocchieschi Courts. It is Gothic in style, with a simple facade adorned with two floors of mullioned. windows and slender marble columns and varied capitals. The story goes that Pia, the daughter of Buonconte Guastelloni and widow of Baldo Tolomei, married Nello Pannocchieschi who, suspecting her of adultery, kept her imprisoned in Castel di Pietro in Maremma, where she eventually died. Dante remembers sad Pia in Canto V of Purgatory.

Further on we come to a little square, where the CHURCH OF ST. PETER AT THE STEPS or IN CASTELVECCHIO stands and which, as the name suggests, is preceded by a huge flight of steps. The Church was constructed in the 13th century and completely re-built in the 18th century, with the result that today nothing remains of the original construction. The facade is adorned with a beautiful door and tympanum, a cornice and brick decoration. Inside the Church we can admire in the one and only nave, which was entirely re-built, a **Madonna** by Rustichino situated on the first altar of the right wall, and the **Flight into Egypt**, a famous painting by Rutilio Manetti (1621) near the main altar. The following works are treasured in the nearby rectory: a « **Madonna** » and « **Santa Lucia and the Archangel Gabriel** », by Sano di Pietro; « **Four Saints** », by Ambrogio Lorenzetti (1344); « **Christ Blessing** », by Giovanni di Paolo and a « **Madonna** », by the Lorenzetti school.

We return to Piazza Postierla and go left down VIA STALLOREGGI, in the Panther District. This street is very interesting because it is lined with ancient buildings that have elegant mullioned windows and beautiful decorations.

At the corner of Via di Castelvecchio, in a tabernacle of the facade of the Bambagini Galletti residence, we find a Pietà fresco by Sodoma, which is commonly known as MADONNA OF THE CROW because, according to the legend, in 1348 the crow carrying the dreaded plague germs that caused so much havoc in Siena fell down dead right in this very spot.

Still in Via Stalloreggi, at number 89-91, we arrive at the house in which Duccio painted his famous Majesty during the years 1308-11. Straight after we come to the **Arch of the Two Gates** belonging to the old city walls that were erected in the 11th century. The front of the arch is decorated with tabernacles bearing frescoes of the « **Ma-**

donna and Saints » by Baldassarre Peruzzi, on the upper right, and a « Madonna and Child » most probably by Memmo Filippucci, situated on the left of the outer front. We go past the arch and, turning left, arrive in PIANO DEI MANTELLINI, where we find the **Palazzo Pollini,** which once belonged to the Celsi family and which today is the property of the Neri family. This residence, which was originally designed by Baldassarre Peruzzi, has an elegant brick facade placed on a scarped footing, with two orders of windows and a richly decorated cornice.

Facing the Pollini Residence is the left flank of the Church of **San Niccolò al Carmine,** from where one can get a splendid view of the Duomo towering above the sloping roofs of the buildings as if on a tray. The church was constructed, together with the adjoining mighty, quadrangular bell-tower and the frësco-adorned Cloister, in the year 1300. However, as the whole architectural complex testifies, the Church was partly transformed in the 16th century by Baldassarre Peruzzi. The interior, formed of a single nave, with an open truss and high ogival windows, preserves its 14th century features. The following art works can be seen along the right wall. At the first altar:

– **Adoration of the Shepherds,** by Duccio and finished by Arcangelo Salimbeni; **Assumption of Mary**, a fragment from a fresco by Gualtieri di Giovanni.

Near the second altar:

– **St. Michael,** a highly praised work by Beccafumi; following this are remnants of a fresco depicting the Annunciated, attributed to Ambrogio Lorenzetti, and another representing the **Madonna and Child,** both of the 14th century.

Opening out before us is the **Chapel of the Sacrament,** with its beautiful altar by Marrina and the **Birth of Mary** by Sodoma. After the Chapel comes a Madonna and Child, known as the **Madonna of the Mantellini,** a panel of the Sienese school but of Byzantine origin, dating from the 13th century. This panel is surrounded by **« Saints »,** the work of Francesco Vanni.

We pass the Sacristy, which is an interesting hall constructed around 1512 by Vannoccio Biringucci and designed by Francesco di Giorgio Martini, and then continue along the wall of the left nave, where we can view the **« Martyrdom of St. Bartholomew »** by Alessandro Casolani (1400) and the **« Ascension of Jesus »** by Gerolamo del Pacchia, near the second altar.

Once out of the Church, we turn right into Via della Diana, so named because of the legendary fountain that the Sienese had erected here in order to exploit a hypothetical subterranean river. Dante remembers the fountain in Canto 13 of Purgatory.

At the crossing of Via San Marco lies the feautiful 18th century facade of the former Oratory of the Madonna of the Rosary, which today acts as the Snail District's meeting hall.

Still in Via San Marco and beyond the old Monastery of Santa Marta, which houses a 16th century church, stands the CHURCH OF ST. PETER AND ST. PAUL, also of the Snail District. The construction dates from the 17th century and is the work of Flaminio del Turco.

Its facade, made of brick, is preceded by a portico, while the interior is in the form of a Greek Cross, with three altars richly decorated in stucco-work; the walls bear the crests of the patrons of the District.

Lying near the right altar is a tabernacle with the **Madonna of the Rosary,** dating from the end of the 13th century; the **Conversation of St. Paul,** a painting by Astolfo Petrazzi can be found near the left altar; instead, near the main altar lies the **Coronation of the Virgin** by Andrea del Brescianino.

On the right of the Pollini Residence, the steep VIA SAN QUIRICO climbs up to a little square overlooking which is the **Chapel of the Prisons of St. Ansano,** which is probably the city's first Baptistry, erected in the 9th century and re-built in 1400, when it was also consecrated.

Situated nearby is a Tower, known as the « **Rocchetta** » (meaning little fortress), perhaps of Roman origin and where, according to legend, St. Ansano was said to have been imprisoned.

In this same street, we can also admire the CHURCH OF THE SAINTS QUIRICO AND GIULITTA, then we descend by way of Via TOMMASO PENDOLA and, at the end of this road we turn right into Via San Pietro. Once past the **Arch of St. Augustine,** or the **Arch Gate,** that stands on the same site of another of the ancient Sienese gates and which once marked the city boundary, we come to the « Prato » of St. Augustine, flanked by the CHURCH OF ST. AUGUSTINE.

CHURCH OF ST. AUGUSTINE – The original structure dates from 1258, but towards the end of the 15th century it was transformed and later renovated in around the mid-18th century by Luigi Vanvitelli.

Even the bright interior, formed of a single nave and in the shape of a Latin cross, was re-built by Vanvitelli in 1755. Among the main art works treasured here, along the righ wall near the first altar we have the « **Communion of St. Gerolamo** » by Astolfo Petrazzi (1631), near the second altar is a valuable « **Crucifixion** » by Perugino (1506), and near the fourth altar, « **Jesus falls under the Cross** », by Ventura Salimbeni (1612). The right transept leads to the **Piccolomini Chapel,** which houses the art treasures of the Church and, in the hall situated opposite is a statue of Pius II, sculptured in 1858 by Giovanni Duprè. Inside the Chapel, placed near the altar, is « **Epi-**

phany », a true masterpiece by Sodoma (1518) that strikes one for the light touch of chiaroscuro and the splendid harmony of colours. The right wall bears a marvellous altar-piece of the Blessed Agostino Novello, painted by Simone Martini in around 1330, which has been temporarily transferred to the Duomo Trust Museum. The centre of the triptych bears the figure of the Blessed Augustine, encircled above by two blessed Augustinian friars; the side panels depict some miracles performed by the Blessed Augustine. The most astounding features of this work are the clear design and elegant composition of the whole. On the left wall we can view **« The Massacre of the Innocents »,** a dramatic painting by Matteo di Giovanni, signed and dated 1482.

Adjoining the Church via a portico is the TOLOMEI NATIONAL BOARDING SCHOOL. which was once the Convent of St. Augustine.

Situated in a small square of the « Prato » (meaning lawn) is the tiny CHURCH OF SAN MUSTIOLA ALLA ROSA that houses, in the halls of the ex-Convent, the Museums of the Academy of Physiocritics, recently constructed and comprising the Geomineralogical and Zoological Museums. The Academy, which was founded in 1691 by P. M. Gabrielli within the University and which is still active today, was inspired by the intellectual movement that germinated in France in the second half of the 18th century and was based on a new arrangement of the economic theory as opposed to that of mercantilism and corporativism. In fact, the Physiocritics supported the importance of production, freedom of exchange and free competition, essential conditions for developing a flourishing economy.

Placed between the little square and the Church of St. Augustine is Via Pier Andrea Mattioli, where we find the Institute and Botanical Gardens, then the road descends to the **Tufi Gate**, a barrel-vault construction dated 1325 and attributed to Angelo di Ventura. Via Tufi, which continues beyond the Gate, leads to the **Misericordia Cemetry** where one can admire a number of valuable sculptures and frescoes, mainly works of modern Sienese artists.

Instead, on the right of the **« Prato of St. Augustine »** lies the entrance to VIA S. AGATA, and further on down the street we come to the **Church of St. Joseph,** which was erected in 1600 by the **Guild of Carpenters** and ceded to the inhabitants of the Wave District in the year 1786. Opposite the Church, which has a beautiful facade in brick dating from 1643, the work of Benedetto Giovanelli, stands the delightful fountain of the District. In fact, each District possesses a little fountain situated in the main street or near the Oratory and usually bears a statuette depicting the District's heraldic emblem. On the Patron's

Feast Day, all the babies born during the year are baptized with the water coming from the District fountain.

The Arch of St. Joseph rises up on the left and from here one can get a surprisingly beautiful view of the panorama: the ancient VIA DUPRE' at the end of which rises up the MANGIA TOWER. We are once again nearing the Campo. We go down Via Duprè and, at the end of the street, we turn into Via del Mercato, which flanks the rear side of the Town Hall. In this way we arrive in the lively and picturesque **« Piazza del Mercato »** (Market Square) set up in 1346 to house the cattle market, which once took place in Piazza del Campo.

The Arch of St. Joseph

ITINERARY 4

Piazza del Mercato (Market Square) - **Church of St. Mary of the Servants - Porta Romana - Church of the Holy Spirit.**

This fourth itinerary will take us on a brief though equally interesting and suggestive tour of the South-eastern quarters of the city.

We start the tour from Market Square or « **Piazza del Mercato** », go up a flight of steps on the left, then walk through a gallery and in this way arrive in **Via Salicotto**, once known as **Via Malcucinato.** This street leads us to Siena's Jewish quarter with its 18th century synagogue and which, at one time, used to be full of ancient blackened houses, steep flights of steps and narrow streets. Standing on the right is the **Oratory of St. James,** of the Tower District, which was erected in the year 1531. The District Museum adjoining the Oratory treasures one of Sodoma's last works entitled The Road to Calvary.

At the end of Via del Salicotto we turn left into **Via San Girolamo** where we can admire the **Church of St. Girolamo,** dating from the 14th century. The interior, of a single nave only, houses between the first and second altars on the right the tombstone of Bishop Bettini, which is the work of Giacomo Cozzarelli (1507). In the main chapel we can view the **Coronation of the Virgin** by Sano di Pietro (1465), and near the third altar on the left is a scene by Marrina containing a **Madonna and Saints** by Giuliano da Firenze (1487). The Convent of the same name has a beautiful cloister, where one can view a magnificent fresco of the **Assumption,** attributed to Bernardino Fungai (1487) and, at the sides, Figures of Saints by Giuliano da Firenze and other frescoes of the late 15th century.

We now continue along Via San Girolamo and enter VIA DEI SERVI until we arrive in Piazza Alessandro Manzoni, where the **Church of St. Mary of the Servants** stands. This church was constructed in the 13th century and later extended; it rises on the summit of a high flight of steps, in a secluded tree-lined square that from its heights dominates the entire city, in fact, from here we can admire the imposing mass of the Duomo with its white and black stripes, the grey mass of the Town Hall and that of the Mangia Tower, which stands out against

the sky. The plain and severe facade of the church has only one portal surmounted by two rose-windows, while the Romanesque bell-tower is adorned with mullioned windows which, higher up the tower, become four-mullioned. Some priceless art works are treasured in the church's interior, which is Renaissance in the naves and Gothic in the transept and apse and whose designs are attributed to Baldassarre Peruzzi of Porrina, while the construction work was carried out by Ventura Turapilli. Near the first pillar on the right we find a beautiful holy-water stoup dating, in part, from the end of the 13th century.

The wall of the right nave bears the remnants of a fresco dating from the 14th century.

Near the second altar: a **Madonna and Child** known as « **Madonna of Bordone** », a masterpiece of Coppo di Marcovaldo.

Near the fifth altar: **Massacre of the Innocents,** by Matteo di Giovanni.

The lunette displays another work by the same artist entitled **Madonna and Saints** (1471), which shows great harmony in the colours and form; on the right is Taddeo di Bartolo's **Adoration of the Shepherds** (1404).

Right arm of the cross-vault: **Madonna and Child** by Segna di Bonaventura this work can be found near the Sacristy door).

The apse of the main altar is flanked by two chapels lying in each arm of the transept. The second chapel on the right of the Presbytery is the most interesting for it houses two priceless works of art on the right wall: **Massacre of the Innocents**, an intensely dramatic painting and one of the best ever done by Pietro Lorenzetti; **Madonna and the People,** one of the most graceful scenes painted by Lippo Memmi.

In the second chapel on the left of the Presbytery we find the following paintings hanging on the right wall: **Herod's Banquet** by Pietro Lorenzetti; **Passage of St. John the Evangelist,** by the same artist. Unfortunately, both these works are rather damaged.

The chapel at the far end of the left transept houses a **Madonna of the Misericordia,** dated 1436 and erroneously signed Giovanni di Pietro; the artist was instead Giovanni di Paolo. Lying near the main altar is Bernardino Fungai's altar-piece representing the **Coronation of the Virgin,** dating from 1500.

The following can be found along the wall of the left nave.

1st altar: the **Annunciation** by Francesco Vanni.

2nd altar: **Madonna of Belvedere,** by Jacopo di Mino del Pellicciaio (1363) and at the sides, **Madonna and St. Joseph** by Bernardino Fungai.

Hanging above the wall of the entrance is a **Crucifix** dating from the 14th century and, perhaps, sculptured by Niccolò di Segna.

The ORATORY OF THE HOLY TRINITY is situated between the apse and the transept of the Church of St. Mary of the Servants, and it looks into **Via Val di Montone.** The Blessed Francesco Patrizi founded the Oratory in 1298, but later, towards the end of the 17th century, it was re-touched.

The interior is adorned with a rich decoration, 16th-17th century, formed of stuccoes by Prospero Brescianino and Cristoforo Rustici and frescoes by Raffaele Vanni, Giuseppe Nasini and Ventura Salimbeni. A bronze **Crucifix** dated 1576, hangs near the altar and in the right chapel we find a **Madonna and Child** by Sano di Pietro, while the tabernacle in the Sacristy houses an exquisite work by Neroccio di Bartolomeo, depicting a **« Madonna and Child and Saints Michael and John the Baptist ».**

Climbing up the flight of steps, we come to VIA ROMA, right in front of the CHURCH OF THE « SANTUCCIO » or SMALL SAINT, dating from 1362 and belonging to the former Monastery of St. Mary of the Angels. Behind the church, there is a building that incorporates the remains of the city walls of 1257, and here we find the Museum of the Society of the Executors of Pious Orders, that was commissioned in 1938. A number of beautiful art works are kept here, to name a few: a reliquary in the form of a triptych, perhaps by Bernardino Fungai, a tabernacle by Ugolino di Nerio and paintings by Niccolò di Ser Sozzo Tegliacci, Sodoma, Giacomo Cozzarelli, Girolamo di Benvenuto and Lippo Memmi.

We continue along Via Roma and arrive at **Porta Romana,** which

Porta Romana

is Siena's most solemn gate adorned with merlons and battlements for defence purposes. Its construction, which dates from 1327, was carried out by Agnolo di Ventura. The outer arch bears the remains of a fresco entitled « **The Coronation of Mary** » which was begun by Taddeo di Bartolo in 1417 and continued first by Sassetta in 1447, then by Sano di Pietro (1459). Instead, underneath the arch we find the one and only fresco painted by Sassetta depicting the **Glory of a Band of Angels.**

Beyond the Gate, lying only a few minutes away, is the Renaissance Church of **St. Mary of the Angels,** dating from the 15th century, which stands in Via Enea Silvio Piccolomini.

We return to Via Roma and walk in the direction of the City centre. On the right we pass the **Church of Refuge,** which was constructed in 1598 and, which has a late-Renaissance marble facade formed of three orders and attributed to B. Giovanelli. The church interior houses paintings by Domenico di Bartolo, Francesco Vanni, Ventura Salimbeni and Rutilio Manetti.

Further on along the same street stands the **St. Galgano Building,** which is Renaissance in style as far as its architecture and the characteristic ashlar-work are concerned. Instead, the two simple and plain orders of mullioned-windows are decidedly Gothic.

We now walk to the end of Via Roma and down **Via Pantaneto,** then, turning right into **Via Pispini** we come to the **Church of the Holy Spirit,** which is a brick construction dating from 1498. The marble portal, which opens out on a simple hut-like facade, dates from the year 1519 and was probably designed by Baldassarre Peruzzi. The massive dome of 1508 is, instead, attributed to Giacomo Cozzarelli.

The church interior has only one nave, which was restored in 1921, a dome situated at the crossing of the arms and a deep Presbytery.

RIGHT WALL – Near the wall of the entrance we find a « Nativity » scene in coloured terra cotta, the work of Friar Ambrogio della Robbia (1509).

1st chapel of the Spagnoli: it is richly adorned with paintings and frescoes by Sodoma, one of the most important artists of Sienese art, who was particularly influenced by Leonardo's painting. Among the paintings there are: **Saints Niccolò da Tolentino** and **Archangel Michael** (altar); the **Virgin** handing the vestments of the Dominican Order to Saint Alfonso (lunette). Among the frescoes there are: **St. Sebastian** (left wall); **St. Anthony the Abbott** (right wall); **San Giacomo da Compostella** (above).

2nd chapel: a beautiful wooden statue by Giacomo Cozzarelli, representing **San Vincenzo Ferreri.**

3rd chapel: the **Coronation of the Virgin** by Domenico Beccafumi.

4th chapel: San Giacinto in Glory, by Francesco Vanni (altar); **Stories of San Giacinto,** by Ventura Salimbeni (wall). Apsidal Vault: **the Pentecost,** fresco by Giuseppe Nasini; Four Saints, the work of Rutilio Manetti (1608, on the pillars of the main altar).

Up above are two simple, but elegantly-made choir stalls.

LEFT WALL – 3rd chapel: a wooden **Crucifix** by Sano di Pietro; two wooden statues attributed to Giacomo Cozzarelli, depicting **« St. Girolamo »** and the **« Madonna ».**

2nd chapel: wooden statue by Cozzarelli, dedicated to St. Catherine of Siena.

1st chapel: « Assumption and the Saints Francis and Catherine of Siena », work attributed to Matteo Balducci (16th century). The Cloister of the ancient Convent of the Dominican Order is a harmonious construction and treasures a Crucifix dated 1516 made by Friar Paolino da Pistoia.

Situated in the little square in front of the church is the Pispini Fountain.

We leave the church and continue along Via Pispini, which follows the red city walls, leaning out from which are the buildings, churches, towers, just like in **« Buongoverno »** (Good government) that Ambrogio Lorenzetti painted in the Town Hall. Beyond the little **Church of San Gaetano,** erected by the inhabitants of the Conch Shell District in 1670-80, at the crossing of Via dell'Oliviera, we arrive at the **Pispini Gate,** formerly called the **San Viene Gate,** because the relics of the First Martyr Ansano were found by a shepherdess near Arbia and brought into Siena via this gate, while the people awaited exclaiming **« The Saint is coming... the Saint is coming! ».** This gate, which was probably erected by Minuccio di Rinaldo in 1326, is

Porta Pispini

adorned with a « **Glory of Angels** », the remnants of a much larger work by Sodoma representing the Nativity (1531).

Once again, we go down Via Pantaneto where the **Church of St. George** stands with its solid and slender Romanesque bell-tower. This church was re-built in 1741 over an earlier construction dating from the 1200, which was built in memory of the Battle of Montaperti.

We turn right into **Via del Porrione** and once past the Brotherhood of the Misericordia, an old society of St. Anthony the Abbot, founded around 1250 by the Blessed Andrea Gallerani, we come to the **Church of St. Martin,** a late-Renaissance work constructed by Giovanni Battista Pelori in 1537.

The facade dating 1613 is by Giovanni Fontana. The entrance to the church is situated at the top of a short flight of steps, while the interior, which is in the shape of a Latin Cross, has a single nave, a huge dome painted with frescoes by Annibale Mazzuoli and, a deep presbytery.

The walls of the interior, as in majority of the Sienese churches, are adorned with finely-decorated marble altars: three on each wall and one on each arm of the cross-vault.

The right wall of the nave. – 2nd altar: **Circumcision,** by Guido Remi (1640). 3rd altar: **Martyrdom of St. Bartholomew,** work of Guercino. It is enclosed within a rich, marble frame of the Lorenzo Marrina school (1522).

Positioned before the 3rd altar are five gilded statues of wood: **Madonna and Child, St. Peter, St. Bartholomew, St. John and St. Anthony the Abbot.** These statues are attributed to Jacopo della Quercia and his pupils and were sculptured during the period 1419-1425.

The right arm of the transept: near the altar lies a statue of Tommaso da Villanova, work of Giovanni Antonio Mazzuoli. Instead, Giuseppe Mazzuoli's other work entitled « **The Conception** » is placed on the altar lying opposite.

The main altar is by Lorenzo Marrina (1522), while the statues of **Angels and Saints** are, once again, by Giuseppe Mazzuoli. The vaults of the apse are richly decorated with frescoes and the beautiful stained-glass window depicting **St. Martin** is the work of Pastorino de' Pastorini.

On the left of the apse is an ogival chapel bearing the remains of some rather deteriorated frescoes.

The left wall of the nave: 3rd altar, by Lorenzo Marrina; **Nativity** by Domenico Beccafumi. 2nd altar: a **Crucifix** between the **Madonna and St. John the Evangelist,** wooden statues of the 15th century. 1st. altar: **St. Ivone,** by Raffaele Vanni.

A panel near the entrance depicts the **Madonna protecting Siena,** and it was carried out by Giovanni di Lorenzo Cini in memory of the Battle of Camollia (1526).

We now come out of the church and continue along Via del Porrione, which further on brings us to Piazza del Campo.

ITINERARY 5

The University - The Papal Loggias - Church of St. Mary of Provenzano - Basilica of St. Francis - Oratory of St. Bernardine - The Ovile Gate - Salimbeni Residence - Tolomei Residence.

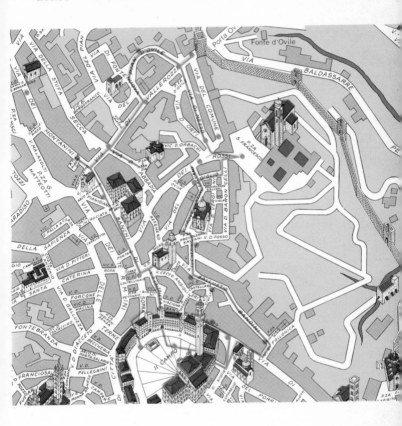

We leave Campo, from the Eastern side of the Square and, entering **Via Banchi di Sotto**, we straightaway come to the aforementioned **Piccolomini Residence** situated at the corner of Via Rinaldini. Standing opposite is the **University,** which since 1815 occupies the former monastery of Saint Virgilius, dating from the 16th century. At the centre of the courtyard we find the MEMORIAL TO THE STUDENTS KILLED AT CURTATONE (29th May, 1848) together with a bronze group sculpture by Raffaello Romanelli (1892). On the left is the TOMB OF NICCOLO' ARINGHIERI, a Reader in Law, the work of an unknown Sienese artist and follower of Goro di Gregorio (1374). At the end of the courtyard are two statues by Pietro Tenerani: one in **Memory of the Mayor** of Siena and the other of GIULIO BIANCHI BANDINELLI.

The Lawyer's Circle Library is housed on the first floor and boasts a collection of well over four hundred thousand books and leaflets.

The Sienese **School of Studies,** which already existed in the early 13th century, is considered one of the oldest in the whole of Italy and was founded by the sheer will of the Commune, without any papal or imperial privileges. It acquired great fame in 1321, when it received the masters and scholars of the Bolognese School of Studies, so much so that Charles V granted it the privileges of a general school of studies in the year 1357. After a period of great splendour, the Sienese School of Studies declined under Leopold I and, from 1809-1814, it ceased all its activities. Later, however ,it was revived thanks to the interest of the private citizens and local bodies and, in 1884, it adopted the system that the University currently maintains. This system comprises the following faculties: Jurisprudence with a degree course in Political Science, Medicine and Surgery, Pharmacy with a degree course in Chemistry and Pharmaceutical Technology, Mathematics, Physics and Natural Science with a degree course in Biology and Geology, Economics and Banking with a degree course in Statistics and Economics, Literature and Philosophy.

A little further on, though still in **Via Banchi di Sotto** and corresponding to the **Church of St. Martin,** we come to the Papal Loggias that were ordered to be erected in 1462 according to Antonio Federighi's project – as stated in the epigraph « PIUS II P. in gentilibus suis Piccolomineis » – by Enea Silvio Piccolomini, who embellished Siena with numerous beautiful buildings and works of art. The great families gathered together in these loggias on important occasions, such as weddings, funerals, grand receptions, along with their friends, workers and town folk. The three elegant arcades, decorated by Francesco di Giorgio Martini, have a smooth upper area that serves as an architrave. This wonderful architecture, so luminous and well-balanced like all the purest features of the Renaissance style, finds a perfect framework in the buildings that look onto the Square.

Following, on the right, is the ancient **Pantaneto Fountain** beyond which one turns left along VIA DI FOLLONICA that leads to a little square where the **Church of St. John the Baptist with the Staff stands**. This church also known as **« San Giovannino »,** belongs to the Horned Lion District and dates from the 13th century, although it was re-built in the 16th century and then restored three centuries later.

From this square we go up along VIA SALLUSTIO BANDINI, one of the most characteristic medieval streets of the city, where one can find the house of the illustrious Sienese man of letters and economist, after whom the street is named.

VIA SAN VIGILIO starts from this point and meets with VICOLO DEL CASTELLARE that leads to the well-preserved, picturesque medieval surroundings of the **Castellare Court of the Ugurgieri.** On the left, along the street of the same name, is the **Church of St. Virgilius,** which was originally of the Camaldoli district, then of the Jesuit and of the Vallombrosani Orders.

But now we come back to Via Bandini and turn right into VIA LUCHERINI that descends in PIAZZA PROVENZANO. Overlooking the end of the square is the beautiful **Church of St. Mary of Provenzano.**

Constructed by Flaminio del Turco, to the designs of the Carthusian Damiano Schifardini, in honour of the miraculous image of the Madonna that is venerated here and which was previously kept in the house of Provenzano Salvani.

Even the Baroque churches harmonise with the architecture of Siena, as in very few other cities, because they are built of red-brick; in other words a sort of Baroque-Renaissance mixture, well-stressed in the balanced geometry of the facades, in the volume of the side flanks, right up to the apse part. The facade, in its simple and grand entirety, is divided into two orders by a heavily projecting cornice. While the dome rises up above a high, octagonal tambour. The following art works can be viewed in the Baroque interior formed of a single nave only.

1st altar: St. Cerbone, by Rutilio Manetti (1630).

Around the dome pillars: four flags, three taken by the Turks in the 17th and 18th centuries and one by the Chinese Boxers in 1901.

On the altar of the right transept: **St. Catherine's Vision,** by Francesco Rustici. Near the main altar, preserved in a richly-decorated tabernacle, is a relief of the venerated image of the **Madonna of Provenzano** (15th century), from which the church takes its name.

The altar in the left transept: **Crucifix between St. Mary Magdalen and St. John the Evangelist,** sculptures of the 17th century.

The Sacristy – 1st room: **the Madonna,** a 14th century fresco by the Sienese school; the **Holy Family,** by Francesco Vanni; and Dedication to the Church, a 16th century painting of interest because it explains the topography of the city. 2nd room: beautiful inlaid closets and a **Pietà** by Cristofano Casolani.

Coming out of the church, we walk along VIA PROVEN-ZANO SALVANI, which flanks the left side, then turning left again, down VIA DEL GIGLIO, we come to the **Church of San Pietro Ovile,** dating from the 13th century but later transformed by restoration work. The church interior houses some priceless works of art: at the right altar lies a beautiful 15th century imitation by Matteo di Giovanni of Simone Martin's famous **Annunciation,** which today is kept in the Uffizi Gallery in Florence. In the apse we find a **Crucifix** by Giovanni di Paolo, while standing near the altar on the left of the main one are two statues of **the Madonna and St. John the Evangelist** by Niccolò of the « Choirs » (1415). Another marvellous work is the Madonna and Child of the so-called Master of San Pietro

Ovile who, according to some, is presumed to be Ugolino Lorenzetti, a follower of Ugolino di Nerio as well as of Pietro Lorenzetti, hence the name taken by the artist.

From the church we go down the street of the same name, which crosses on the right with VIA DEI ROSSI, a street filled with 13th and 14th century red-brick buildings; here the houses form a sort of screen cut open by the tiny streets and alleys that all bear names worthy of a novel by Sacchetti or Boccaccio, such as « **Via del Refe Nero** » (Black Thread Street).

At the end of this street, which is suitable only for walking in and where the residents live in close contact with one another, amidst the noise and amiable chatter on household topics, we come to the **St. Francis Arch** with its 14th century marble statues and the Madonna by Tino di Camaino that dominates the summit. Beyond the arch is a spacious square from where one can view another beautiful panorama of Siena: the rosy complex of the second largest church of Siena together with St. Dominic, the BASILICA OF ST. FRANCIS.

BASILICA OF ST. FRANCIS – It was begun in 1326 in the Gothic style, over the site of another church that once existed and was terminated in 1475, probably following the project of Francesco di Giorgio Martini. However, in 1665, the church was devastated by a fire and was restored though in the Baroque style. Thanks to Giuseppe Partini, it was given back its original aspect during the period 1885-1892. The present facade in brick, carried out in 1894-1913 by Vittorio Mariani and Gaetano Ceccarelli and brightened by portions in marble, has a beautiful portal decorated with statues, high-reliefs in the lunette, various coats-of-arms, an elaborate rose-window with symbols of the Evangelists, and a tympanum. The bell-tower, dating 1765, is the work of Paolo Rosi.

The extremely beautiful interior is in the form of an Egyptian Cross and has a wide single nave, with white and black alternate stripes on the walls and an open truss-work ceiling, while illuminating the interior are mullioned windows and huge stained-glass windows in the apse.

The church possesses works of great artistic value: on the right of the entrance are fragments of a 14th century tomb. The first lunette of the right wall depicts the « **Visitation and Saints** », early 15th century frescoes and other Saints of the 14th century Sienese school. The Tomb of Tolomei with a tombstone lies after the side door and, according to legend, it is said to contain the **sepulchre of Pia Tolomei.**

From the Sacristy, with its pretty 16th century basin and frescoes of Angels by Sodoma, we pass into a chapel of the former convent.

The right transept: at the head of the arm lies a statue of **St. Francis** attributed to Francesco di Valdambrino.

2nd chapel: on the right of the presbytery: the tomb of **Cristoforo Felici,** by Urbano da Cortona (1462).

1st chapel: Madonna and Child, by Andrea Vanni.
Left wall of the presbytery: two medallions bearing the portraits of Vittoria Forteguerri and Silvio Piccolomini, the parents of Pius II.
The left transept: 1st chapel: **Crucifixion,** a detached fresco by Pietro Lorenzetti.
3rd chapel: frescoes by Ambrogio Lorenzetti, one depicting « **San Ludovico d'Angiò before Bonifacio VIII** », on the right wall, and the other representing the « **Martydom of six Franciscan friars at Ceuta** », on the left wall.
6th chapel: a graffiti flooring by Marrina.
An open doorway situated on the left flank, leads to the harmonious square cloister. According to an ancient legend, the stairway descending here is said to treasure the remains of 18 nobles of the Tolomei family, who were killed by the same number of nobles of the Salimbeni family during a banquet on the hills near Siena, today still nicknamed « **Malamerenda** » meaning to bad dinner. From the cloister we pass on to the Seminary that preserves a marble bas-relief of the Madonna and Child, probably the work of Giacomo Cozzarelli, together with a fresco of the Madonna and Saints by Lippo Vanni.
On the right side of the basilica stands the former **Convent of St. Francis,** erected in the 15th century and extended in 1518. It is currently undergoing restoration work as it is destined to house the University's Banking and Economic Science Faculty.

On the right side of the St. Francis Square we also find the **Oratory of St. Bernardine,** which was erected in the 15th century over the same site where St. Bernardine used to preach. This Saint, who was born in Massa Marittima in 1380 and died in Aquila in 1444, studied Humanities and Law in Siena before entering the Franciscan Order at the age of 22 years. He started preaching in Genoa and this vocation took him round almost the whole of Northern and Central Italy, where he became well-known for his fresh and modern approach. In fact, the Franciscan Order considered him a providential reformer and to the Catholic faith he proved the creator of a new spiritual fervour that was to influence both the religious and town life of his period.

The Oratory consists of two floors, the **Upper and Lower Oratories** wherein are treasured art works of notable interest. First we shall visit the Lower Oratory that is decorated with 17th century paintings.
Near the altar is a « **Madonna and Child and the Saints Bernardine and Ansano** », by Brescianino, while the side niches of the altar contain two statues of **St. Bernardine and St. Catherine,** painted in white and dating from the 16th century. At the upper floor, the lunette above the entrance door of the vestibule bears a painted wooden **Madonna and Child,** of the Jacopo della Quercia school; near the vestibule altar we find a **Madonna** by Sano di Pietro; a glass case on the left contains a gonfalon painted by Francesco Vanni, while the niche on the right has

Madonna and Child (Sano di Pietro)

a delicate bas-relief by Giovanni d'Agostino, depicting the
Madonna and Child on a throne and two Angels.

The Upper Oratory is more interesting with the ceiling and
walls in wood and decorated with stuccoes done by Ventura
Turapilli in 1496. Situated between the pillars are extremely
valuable frescoes. Starting from the left corner of the wall
opposite the entrance, we have: **St. Ludovico** by Sodoma; the
Birth of Mary by Girolamo del Pacchia; the **Presentation of
Mary at the Temple** by Sodoma; a **Marriage Ceremony** by
Domenico Beccafumi; **St. Bernardine and the Archangel Gabriel
Annunciating,** by Girolamo del Pacchia. On the other side we
have the **Annunciated** again by Girolamo del Pacchia. In the

The Oratory of St. Bernardine

middle: the **Virgin in Glory surrounded by Saints**, by Domenico Beccafumi; **St Anthony of Padua** and the **Visitation** by Sodoma; **Mary's Transit** by Domenico Beccafumi; **the Assumption and St. Francis of Assisi,** by Sodoma and probably the Oratory's most beautiful fresco. Hanging between the windows in front of the altar, is Sodoma's **Coronation of Mary.**
Preserved here are relics of the heart of St. Bernardine and the Panel venerated by him bearing the monogram of Jesus.

Coronation of Mary (Sodoma)

We leave the Oratory, pass by the St. Francis Arch, go down Via dei Rossi and then, from here, we turn right into Via del Comune, which is one of the most lively and characteristic of the Sienese streets like VIA DI MEZZO and VIA DEGLI ORTI that lie parallel and slope steeply downhill.

Walking along Via del Comune we come to the **Oratory of the Visitation,** dating from the year 1600 and belonging to the Caterpillar District. After the Oratory comes the **Oville Gate,** which is 14th century and has a battlement. A tabernacle situated in the left wall bears a fresco of the Madonna and Child painted by Sano di Pietro. Beyond the Gate and down the flight of steps which give access to a little vale, we find the **Ovile Fountain** created in 1262 and situated in a very picturesque site against a background of vineyards and hills just outside the city walls.

Once again, as in many other occasions, we cannot help but admire these characteristics so typical of Siena: the variety of city and country which follow one another so naturally and, in this same natural way, the very particular mixture of houses and buildings sprang up on the three Tuscan hills. For example, behind a church stretching out in steps is a vineyard and, at the end lies a fountain. Climbing up the hill ridge amongst farm houses, at the top we can expect to find a residence, a loggia, a tower, all of splendid architecture demostrating the arrival point of a very refined civilization. Behind these houses are cypresses, holm-oaks, orchards and wide fields, which give us the possibility of scenting once again the natural odour of the farmland. Similar to a gigantic San Gimignano, where lying at intervals we find nature, churches and houses all in continuous contact with one another.

On the left of the fountain, walking down **Via di Fonte Nuova,** we come to VIA DI VALLEROZZI wherein stands the delightful **Church of St. Rocco,** an early 16th century construction belonging to the She-Wolf District. In fact, a column bearing a reproduction of the Sienese she-worf stands in front of the church.

The church interior is adorned with paintings by 17th century Sienese artists and one of the chapels contains the « **Stories of St. Rocco** » by Rutilio Manetti.

From Via dei Rossi, we arrive on the right in **Via dell'Abbadia** and then come to the square looking onto which is the rear side of the **Salimbeni Residence,** constructed in brick with two mighty turrets at each side; this rear part of the building, which dates from the 14th century, is considered much more characteristic than the facade.

Standing in front is the **Church of San Donato,** which was erected in 1119 as the St. Michael Abbey and then passed over to the Carmelite Order in 1683 who transformed it greatly. It was finally reduced to a simple parish church under its present name.

The only parts which have been preserved of the origina construction are the hut-like stone and brick facade and the lower half of the apse. While the single-naved interior preserves the ancient high cupola supported by ogival arches and well-shafts. At the upper right one can view the remains of a 14th century fresco by the Sienese school and a **Madonna and Child** by Luca Tommè. The main altar is adorned with a tabernacle and Angels sculptured by Giuseppe Mazzuoli and the apse has a fresco by Luigi Ademollo depicting St. Michael.

The 18th century **Oratory of the Holy Nails** next door to the church displays inside other coffin heads by Riccio and a **Madonna** by Andrea Vanni lying near the altar of the following chapel.

Continuing along Via dell'Abbadia we reach VIA DI VALLEROZZI which then ascends to VIA DEI MONTANINI. Here we come across the **Oratory of St. Mary of the Snows,** attributed to Francesco di Giorgio Martini (1471), with its elegant Renaissance facade adorned with a rather deteriorated portal, while the interior is very plain and illuminated by extremely small windows. Near the altar is the Madonna of the Snows, Matteo di Giovanni's masterpiece dated 1477.

Via dei Montanini leads through two medieval towers into **Salimbeni Square,** which is flanked on three sides by monumental buildings, while at the centre stands a statue of **Sallustio Bandini,** Tito Sarrocchi's sculpture dated 1882.

At the end of the square we can view the facade of the **Salimbeni Residence** whose Gothic building, dating from the 14th century, was extended and restored in 1879 by Giuseppe Partini. It consists of three floors, the middle one having six elegant three-mullioned windows with ogival arches that frame the noble families' coats-of-arms. This building is the head office of MONTE DEI PASCHI DI SIENA, the oldest Bank in Italy, which was founded in 1624 as a Credit Bank, because it had as its capital the annual income from the government-owned Sienese Maremma Pastureland.

On display in the interior are the ancient stores of the Salimbeni family as well as the Bank's archives, containing seals, administration books and other important documents pertaining to the economic history of Siena. The administration halls are richly embellished with numerous works of both ancient and modern art for example, a marble statue of **Bacco** by Antonio Federighi, a huge Pietà fresco by Riccio, a Madonna and Child in marble by Antonio Rossellino, a Madonna by Giovanni di Paolo and a wooden statue of a Saint, attributed to Pietro d'Angelo.

The Spannocchi Residence, situated on the right side of the square, is an elegant, Renaissance style building whose construction was begun in 1470 by Giuliano da Maiano for Pius II's treasurer, Ambrogio Spannocchi, and then completed by Giuseppe Partini in 1880.

Standing opposite, on the left side of the square is the **Tantucci Residence,** again Renaissance in style and designed by Riccio (1548).

Walking further down Via Banchi di Sopra, we can admire the **Gori Pannilini Residence,** the Gothic brick **Cinughi Residence,** the **Bichi Ruspoli Residence** dating from 1520, today the head office of the Banca Nazionale dell'Agricoltura (National Bank of Agriculture), which is flanked on either side by two ancient shortened towers.

The street then widens into **Tolomei Square,** with a column bearing the tin sculpture of a she-wolf, made by Domenico Arrighetti in 1620. Here we find the **Tolomei Residence,** which is solid, compact and geometric and is the most stable and ancient building in Siena. It already existed before 1205, then, with the exception of the ground floor, it was re-built after 1267. The other facade consists of two floors, adorned with elegant mullioned windows and three-lobed arcades. But let's walk around the building, from the tiny street bordering it, until the street running parallel with the Square: this building is a complete block of solid stone and represents that other face of Siena, not the gay and mystic one but the Romanesque and warring Siena, firm and indestructible in defending the freedom so dear to her people. Recently the building underwent some admirable restoration work and today it is the head office of the Cassa di Risparmio di Firenze (Saving's Bank of Florence).

Facing the Tolomei building is the **Chuch of St. Christopher,** of Romanesque origin, but completely re-built in the 18th century. The Council of the Republic used to meet here before the construction of the Town Hall.

The brick facade is adorned with two statues by Giuseppe Silini, dedicated to the Blessed Bernardo and Nera Tolomei, who lived during the 13th century.

In the single-naved interior we can admire: a wooden crucifix bound in leather, considered a unique work of the 14th century, while in the following span we find two panels of an altar-piece attributed to Sano di Pietro and depicting **St. Christopher and St. George killing the Dragon.** The hall on the right of the presbytery bears a 15th century terra cotta of **St. Galgano** by the Antonio Federighi school. Bartolomeo Mazzuoli's marble group sculpture depicting the **Blessed Bernardo Tolomei** adorns the main altar.

Situated on the left flank of the church, in **Via del Moro,** bordered on the left by the **Palmieri Nuti Residence,** is the entrance to a small, but interesting brick cloister, which was constructed in the 12th century behind the Romanesque apse of St. Christopher. Very little remains of the ancient construction, only two sides of a small, modest loggia in brick tiles, however it is considered an opening into Siena's past which has remained at a stand still over the centuries and preserves the rhythm of that distant life.

From Tolomei Square we go along **Via Banchi di Sopra** until we return to Piazza del Campo.

ITINERARY 6

Piazza del Campo - Academy of the Rozzi - Via Galluzza - Branda Fountain - House and Sanctuary of St. Catherine - Basilica of St. Dominic - National Archeological Museum - Camollia Gate - Medici Fortress - The Italian Wine Cellar.

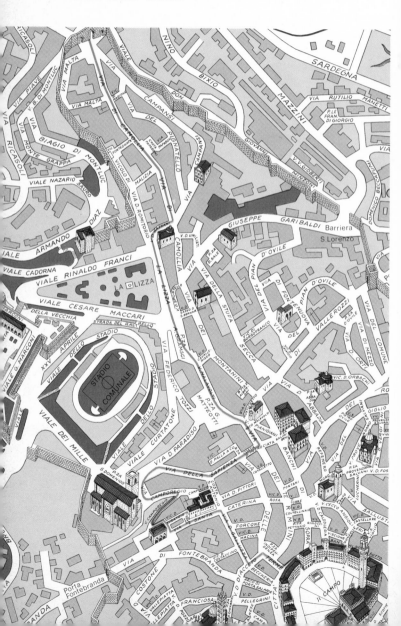

And now we start our sixth and last itinerary. From Piazza del Campo we once again climb up to Via di Città and, after having turned right into VIA DELLE TERME, we arrive in PIAZZA INDIPENDENZA (Independence Square), where we can admire the **Academy of the « Rozzi »** (meaning course mannered).

It was founded in Siena in 1531 by a group of artisans who opposed the **Intronati Academy,** which admitted Sienese aristocrats, scholars and men of letters from all over Italy, and was first known as the **« Congrega »** or **Band of the Rozzi;** only in 1691 the name was changed to Academy of the Rozzi. Given its very popular and anti-academic aspect, this academy directed its activities mainly in the theatrical sector. In fact, close by stands the **Theatre of the Rozzi,** constructed in 1816 to the designs of Alessandro Doveri and restored a few decades later. In this square we also find the **Loggia of Independence,** the work of Archimede Vestri and dating from 1887.

Behind the loggia stands the medieval **Ballati Residence,** crowned with merlons and dominated by a rectangular stone tower. From the square we turn left into VIA DIACCETO, then right into VIA GALLUZZA, which is perhaps the most characteristic street of Siena, for it is flanked by well-preserved medieval houses and spanned by eight arches, the first of which is adorned with an elegant three-mullioned window.

The Branda Fountain and the Basilica of St. Dominic

Straight away on the left lies the steep alley which is typically medieval, Sienese and enchanting, namely VIA DI COSTACCINA. This alley leads us to Via Fonte Branda, at the end of which lies the **Branda Fountain,** the most famous of all the Sienese fountains, which dates from 1081, later extended by Bellamino and re-done in 1246 by Giovanni di Stefano.

Its name is probably derived from a house that stood nearby, which was the property of a certain BRANDO or ILDEBRANDO, or perhaps from the ancient BRANDI family. It is made of brick tiles and the front consists of three great ogival arches, surmounted by tympanums and decorated with merlons, and four lion-shaped gargoyles protecting at the centre the coat-of-arms of Siena. Above the fountain overhangs the apsidal part of the Basilica of St. Dominic.

124

House and Sanctuary of St. Catherine – Further down via Fontebranda we come to the dreary VIA DEL TIRATOIO where the actual **house of St. Catherine** stands. In this house, with its beautiful Renaissance portal made of stone and the delightful loggia in brick, lived Caterina Benincasa (1347-1380), an energetic and passionate interpreter of the cause for modernizing the Church, free from political and national ties and dedicated to the mission for universal freedom. She was the daughter of Jacopo of the Wool Guild and Monna Lapa di Puccio Piagenti, and she proved one of the most fervent and active figures in her period. Her mysticism and indestructible faith made her one of the highest examples of Christianity and, at the same time, an important personality in history. Just think, it was thanks to her that Pope Gregory XI was induced into bringing the Papal Seat from Avignon back to Rome in 1337.

St. Catherine was canonized in 1461 by Pope Pius II and in 1939 proclaimed co-Patron of Italy. Upon her canonization, the Sienese people began work on restoring and consecrating the house of St. Catherine, which was later turned into a **Sanctuary**.

House of St. Catherine

This brought about changes to the house's original structure: in fact, the **Lower Oratory** was created over the site where the Saint's father had his laundry; the Upper Oratory or of the Kitchen; the Oratory of the Crucifix where the vegetable garden stood, and the Oratory of the Little Room which was the actual room of St. Catherine.

We shall go straight up to the **Upper Oratory,** which has a lacunar ceiling with gilded rosettes. It was restored in 1594 to Riccio's designs.

The beautiful flooring of majolica has 3,061 tiles of different designs, work of the potter Girolamo di Marco, dating from the year 1600.

Near the altar we find a painting by Bernardo Fungai that depicts **St. Catherine with the stigmata.** The walls above the beautiful Renaissance stalls are covered with the following paintings.

On the left of the altar: **Jesus shows the Saint the cross donated to a poor person,** by the Sodoma school.

Left wall: **the Blessed Ambrogio Sansedoni,** by Gaetano Marinelli (1865); **Two Condemned who were converted by the Saint's prayers,** by Lattanzio Bonastri di Lucignano (1589); **The Saint's Communion,** by Pomarancio; The **Saint frees a person possessed,** by Pietro Sorri; the **Blessed Giovanni Colombini,** by Alessandro Casolani.

Wall in front of the altar: **Jesus changes his heart for that of the Saint,** probably by Francesco Vanni and, above, **The Saint enlightened by the Holy Spirit,** by Rutilio Manetti.

The lunette: **the Saint being canonized,** by Francesco Vanni; on the side: **the Saint receives the crown of thorns from Jesus,** again by Francesco Vanni; and above: **the Saint has a vision of Jesus at the pillar,** by Rutilio Manetti.

Right wall: the **Blessed Andrea Gallerani,** by Francesco Vanni; the **Saint persuades the people of Rome to remain faithful to Pope Urbano VI,** by Alessandro Casolani; **Gregory XI returns the Papal Seat to Rome,** by Pomerancio; the **Mystic Wedding of St. Catherine,** by Arcangelo Salimbeni (1579); **St. Bernardine,** by Pietro Aldi (1865).

Right side of the altar: **the Saint donates a tunic to a poor person,** by the Sodoma school.

Coming out we walk through the elegant loggia, attributed to Baldassarre Peruzzi and restored by G. B. Pelori in 1553, and then enter the Oratory of the Crucifix situated in front, which was so named because in 1632, the 13th century crucifix on a panel by the Pisan school that had been taken from the Church of St. Christine of Pisa, was installed here and it is even believed that the Saint received the stigmata before the Crucifix; the latter can be found near the altar.

The Oratory is decorated with frescoes, the majority of which by Giuseppe Nasini; instead, on the left altar we find « **The Apotheosis of St. Catherine** », by Rutilio Manetti, while the one on the right has a painting of **St. Catherine and Gregory XI,** by Sebastiano Conca.

We come back to the entrance and then go into the Oratory of the Saint's Room, on the right, where the Saint used to pray and wait to receive the famous personalities of her era.

On the walls we find the frescoes by Alessandro Franchi (1896) relating the « **Seven Stories of St. Catherine** »; instead, near the altar is a work by Girolamo di Benvenuto depicting « St. Catherine receiving the stigmata ».

A little cubicle nearly contains some of the Saints personal articles: little bottles of aromatic potions for the sick and a piece of her walking stick. Here we can also view the small window, which is kept shut, through which the Saint distributed offerings to the poor and, also, the rock that served as her pillow. Descending again, on the right we enter the **Church of St. Catherine in Via Fontebranda,** or the **District Oratory,** founded by Jacopo Banincasa, which today belongs to the Goose District. It consists of a single room with a cross-vault and treasured here are a wooden statue of St. Catherine, sculptured by Neroccio, with five angels above it, the work of Sodoma and, higher up, near the altar, hangs a painting by Girolamo del Pacchia dedicated to St. Catherine. Two frescoes by Girolamo del Pacchia can be viewed on the right wall, while the left wall has paintings by Vincenzo Tamagni and Ventura Salimbeni, all relating to stories of the Saint's life.

Another hall on the right contains a wooden statue of St. Catherine probably dating from the 13th century.

Continuing along Via Santa Caterina, we turn left into Costa S. Antonio and, walking through a low-ceilinged portico in brick, we arrive in the wide square of PIAZZA SAN DOMENICO (St. Dominic Square). Here we can view the mighty complex of the BASILICA OF ST. DOMINIC, which dominates the hillside and at the foot of which lies the Branda Fountain.

Sanctuary of St. Catherine

BASILICA OF ST. DOMINIC – This Basilica is in the severe Gothic style and made of brick; construction work was started in 1226 by the Dominican Order, who built the nave over a rectangular foundation and the roof in open truss-work. The crypt was built around the year 1300 and given its wide structure, it was considered a real church, so much so that it was named Church « Down Under » or Church of the Dead, because it contained tombs. St. Catherine's relatives were buried here.

In 1340, the square bell-tower in brick was erected over the church and, much later in 1700, it was shortened to its present proportions. Construction work of the Basilica erected in 1465 continued in the 16th century. It was seriously damaged by a fire in 1532 and an earthquake in 1779, however, it underwent restoration work and its original features have been restored.

The facade was never terminated, so as not to change in any way the already-existing Chapel of the Vaults, which jutted out externally, forming a rectangular projection. Situated on the left hand side of this were niches containing the tombs of noble families. Instead, opening out on the right is the 15th century cloister, which has been re-built completely, and where some frescoes have

St. Catherine (Andrea Vanni)

been uncovered attributed to the artists Lippo Memmi and Andrea Vanni.

We enter the Basilica via the door on the right flank and view the interior, formed in the shape of an Egyptian cross and comprising of one nave only, which treasures some interesting and valuable art works.

Two wide arcades situated at the far end of the nave give access to the **Chapel of the Vaults,** which was restored in 1952 and which displays cross-vaults, hence its name. Here in 1363 St. Catherine donned the vestments of the Tertiaries of the Dominican Order and here too, we can view the pillar against which the Saint often leaned during her spiritual « kidnappings ». Near the column of the altar we find Andrea Vanni's fresco of **St. Catherine of Siena,** considered the only authentic portrait of Caterina Benincasa in existence; the wall at the far end bears Mattia Preti's « **Canonization of the Saint** ».

Right Wall – 1st altar: the **Virgin's apparition to the Blessed Andrea Gallerani,** by Stefano Volpi; followed by a 14th century wooden **Crucifix** and a 16th century group sculpture of the Pietà in terra cotta. 2nd altar: **Birth of Mary,** by Alessandro

Casolani (1584) and up above, a 15th century cusped plate depicting **St. Bernardine.**

The **Chapel of St. Catherine** is rich in works of art. The upper part of the arch over the entrance is adorned with two frescoes by Sodoma depicting the Saints Luca and Girolamo, while the lower part has two oil paintings of the Blessed Raimondo da Capua and Tommaso Nacci, done by Francesco Vanni.

A beautiful **marble tabernacle** by Giovanni di Stefano (1466) containing the Saint's head, can be found near the altar. Flanking this are two works by Sodoma (1526) of exceptional artistic value; on the right « **The Ecstasy of St. Catherine** » and on the left « **The Saint Fainting** ». On the left wall we have Sodoma's painting « **The Saint interceding to save a tortured person's soul** », while on the right wall « **The Saint frees a person possessed** », an oil painting by Francesco Vanni (1593). The decorations on the pillars and the 16th century marble flooring are also of great interest.

Beyond the chapel, near the entrance door to the Sacristy, we find a work entitled « **Adoration of the Shepherds** » by Francesco di Giorgio Martini and, in the lunette is a **Pietà** by Matteo di Giovanni with a predella by Bernardino Fungai.

We descend from the left side into the crypt, which acts as a partial foundation of the Basilica. It was constructed in the early 14th century and restored in 1935, has a wide cross-vault and huge windows with modern stained-glass by Fiorenzo Joni.

The Chapel of St. Catherine

Swooning of St. Catherine (Sodoma)

A large Cross painted by Sano di Pietro stands near the main altar and along the left nave we come to the chapel containing a huge plate, by Sodoma and his helpers, depicting the Eternal and Four Saints; also included in this work is another plate depicting the Madonna which is attributed to either Paolo di Giovanni Fei or Francesco Vannuccio (second half of the 14th century). Lying at the far end of the nave is a Crucifivion and Saints, by Ventura Salimbeni and placed on the altar of the right nave is a wooden statue of St. Anthony the Abbot, probably the work of Turino di Sano.

Right Transept – 3rd chapel: **Madonna and Child and Saints,** a monochrome sketch of the early 16th century. 2nd chapel (called the Tedeschi chapel): **tombs of the Tedeschi family,** mainly university students who died in Siena in the 16th century. Some latin epigraphs placed here clearly demonstrate the affection for Italian art and culture.

1st chapel: **Madonna and Child and the Saints Jeremy and John the Baptist,** by Matteo di Giovanni.

Main Altar – The extremely interesting, marble ciborium is by Benedetto da Maiano, who also sculptured the enchanting shapes of the angels on the candle-sticks fixed on the chapel wall (1475).

Left Transept – 1st chapel: **Madonna and Child,** by Sano di Pietro. 2nd chapel: **« St. Barbara enthroned between Angels and Saints Magdalen and Catherine »** and, up above **« Epiphany »** by Matteo di Giovanni (1479). **« Madonna and Child and Four Saints »**, with a **« Pietà »** above, by Benvenuto di Giovanni (1483). 3rd chapel: a 15th century wooden Crucifix.

Lying on the left, at the head of the cross-vault, is a grand monument by Enea Becheroni (1855), which is dedicated to Giuseppe Pianigiani.

Left Wall – 4th altar: **« Madonna and Child, St. John the Baptist and Knight genuflecting »**, a detached fresco by Pietro Lorenzetti.

3rd altar: **« St. Anthony the Abbot frees a person possessed »**, by Rutilio Manetti.

2nd altar: **« Mystic Wedding of St. Catherine of Alexandria »**, by a follower of Alessandro Casolani.

1st altar: **St. Giacinto,** by Francesco Vanni, in a Renaissance style marble framework.

From the square in front of the church, we descend into VIA DELLA SAPIENZA, and after Costa di S. Antonio, on the right, we find the **Intronati Library**, founded in 1759 by the Archdeacon Sallustio Bandini. The **Intronati Academy,** which some say was founded in 1525 and others 1527, came into existence mainly with literary aims and, later, dedicated its activities to the theatre and music.

Ercole Drei's bust sculpture of the Sienese Tozzi (1883-1920) can be viewed in the Library reading room.

This Library has a precious collection of ancient volumes, incunabula and manuscripts of which the most interesting are: Paul's Epistle in Latin (11th century); a Roman Missal ordered to be written by Enea Silvio Piccolomini in 1456; a Roman pontificial of the 15th century decorated with French miniatures; among the incunabula are the Monte Santo di Dio (1477) and Dante with designs by Botticelli (1481); St. Catherine's Letter; an interesting note-book belonging to Francesco di Giorgio Martini with architectural designs and another with military equipment; a famous diary of Giuliano da Sangallo, also containing architectural designs; Byzantine gospel book of the 10th century, coming from the Emperor's Palace at Constantinople and adorned with enamel work and gold-leavers; an 8th century papyrus from Ravenna; an antiphonary in illuminated manuscript by Giovanni di Paolo; a Sienese Franciscan breviary in illuminated manuscript by Sano di Pietro; a very valuable Book of Hours in illuminated manuscript by the Florentine Filippo di Corbizzi (1494).

NATIONAL ARCHEOLOGICAL MUSEUM

At number 1 of the same street we find the Art Institute which houses the NATIONAL ARCHEOLOGICAL MUSEUM founded in 1956. The Institute's first collection was that of Bargagli Petrucci and later the Bonci Casuccini and the

Chigi-Zondadari collection were added. The museum houses objects coming from Chiusi, Chianciano, Montepulciano, Sarteano, Volterra, Castelluccio della Foce, Cetona and the Siena suburbs, and its aim is to document the evolution of civilization that took place in the Sienese territory from the prehistoric to Roman times.

The three sections, Prehistoric, Topographic and Numismatic, occupy eleven halls of the museum.

The first hall displays bones, casts, weapons and articles dating from the Palaeolithic to the Iron age, while the halls numbering from the second to the tenth are dedicated to the Etruscan and Roman periods, from the 7th century B.C. to the 3rd century A.D. The eleventh hall contains the Numismatic section, which comprises an interesting collection of coins from Etruria, Piceno, Umbria, Lazio, Rome uptil Claudio Albino (193-194 A.D.

We shall mention some of the most interesting pieces:

HALL 2: stone sculpture of a crouched lion (5th century B.C.); a xoanon statue in travertine of the female torso (4th century B.C.).

HALL 3: terracotta urn with Eteocle and Polinice; little « oinochoe » with the black figures of Dionysus and Satyr; « Kythos » from Attica, with black figures of a youth rising out of a sacrificial vase with a lit fire underneath (4th century B.C.); « Stammos » from Attica, with red figures of women gathering fruit from the trees (480 B.C. circa).

HALL 4: material dating from the Classical period and originating from the tomb chambers of the Santo Pollinari Estate, with Helen, a handmaiden and Dioscuri, and a mirrored shrine decorated with the embossed figures of Ulysses, Penelope and Argo the dog (end of 5th and early 4th century B.C.).

HALL 5: Etruscan urns in alabaster, originating from the « CUMERE » family tomb, of the Tombs Estate: the first one is particularly interesting for it shows the two brothers Eteocles and Polinice who killed one another in a duel for the throne of Thebes (3rd-1st century B.C.).

- a Roman sarcophagus with lion-hunting scenes (3rd century A.D.
- a sarcophagus of the Chigi « Muses », so named because it comes from the Chigi villa at Cetinale near Siena. This sarcophagus is a Roman imitation probably of the Hadrian period and copied from a Greek original dating from the 4th century B.C.

HALL 5: a small terra cotta urn showing heroes fighting with ploughs; an Etruscan urn in terra cotta depicting scenes of farewell. Etruscan bronzes, among which a warrior with armour and helmet; a « skyphos » in metallic paint decorated with a painting of two swans between palm trees.

HALL 7: Seneca's head: a portrait of a very famous character, and quite a number of copies were made of the same subject. This is a Roman copy that was found in Siena, of the Hellenic original dated 23rd century B.C.; an amphora with black figures of a warrior in a chariot, maenads and satyrs; a chalice-type wide basin with a centaur and seahorse; Adriadne's head, a terra cotta of the 1st century B.C.; a bronze open-work buckle with the figure of a fawn (7th-6th century B.C.; Ephebe in the act of breaking in a horse (5th century B.C.); Ephebe with the sacrificial knife (1st century B.C.).

HALL 8: Black and grey Etruscan vases, amongst which a « holkion » bearing the figures of monsters and panther heads.

HALL 9: Etruscan shrine with rings and swan heads (8th-7th century B.C.); Hellenic clay basins with designs of grape bunches; fragment of a multicoloured cornice decoration in the shape of Acteloo's head (4th-3th century B.C.).

HALL 10: Egyptian statues and Etruscan bronzes.

Straight after the Museum, at the corner of Via delle Terme, lies the **Church of St. Pellegrino of Learning,** erected over the site of an ancient chapel dedicated to St. Mary of the Misericordia, which already existed in 1240. The Blessed Andrea Gallerani saw to the church's extension in 1321, then in 1767 the building was given its present aspect. Recently, it was restored further.

The facade is simple in its design, while the interior comprises a vestibule and nave adorned with Baroque decorations and ivory-white stuccoes. Giuliano Traballesi's **« Stories of the Virgin »** cover the vault up above. Along the right wall are a small ivory and wooden tabernacle of the 14th century, enclosed in a niche, a graphite **Crucifix** of the same period, a panel depicting the Blessed Andrea Gallerani, done by a follower of Taddeo di Bartolo (15th century?) and St. Peter (one of Lippo Memmi's pupils). Near the altar we find a painting of the **Birth of the Madonna,** by Giuseppe Nasini, while hanging along the left wall are: **St. Peter,** by a follower of Lippo Memmi; **St. Paul at Areopago**, by Alessio Calvi; and **St. Pellegrino,** by an unknown artist. The niches contain 18th century statues, some of which are the work of Giuseppe Mazzuoli.

Continuing along Costa dell'Incrociata and then to the right along Via dei Termini, turning right again a little further on, we come into Via dei Montanini, in front of the **Oratory of St. Mary of the Snows,** which is attributed to Francesco di Giorgio Martini. Constructed in 1470-71 and commissioned by Giovanni Cinughi, the Bishop of Pienza and Montalcino, this Oratory has an elegant Renaissance facade, a bell-tower and a polygon-shaped apse. The interior which is very simple and illuminated by delicate windows, contains a beautiful altar-piece near the altar, considered one of Matteo di Giovanni's masterpieces (1477); a **Madonna and Child, Angels and Saints Peter, Jeremy, Lawrence and Catherine,** called **Madonna of the Snow,** because a Saint offered the Virgin a basin full of snow. The predella is painted with three stories that relate the legend of the origin of the Basilica of St. Mary the Elder in Rome: the snow that bordered the basilica area (1st panel); Pope Liberius starts the construction work (2nd panel); Pope Liberius consecrates the basilica (3rd panel).

We continue down Via dei Montanini which forms the

A romantic night view from San Domenico

axis of the Tertiary of Camollia and passes between ancient buildings, such as the beautiful **Costantini Residence,** formerly known as the **Ciaia Residence,** dating from the 15th century.

On the left we meet Via del Cavallerizzo where, at the crossing of Piazza Gramsci, stands the **Coli Residence,** once known as FRANCESCONI-MOCENNI, dating from 1563, but left unfinished.

Further ahead, on the right, we come to the **Church of St. Andrew,** Romanesque in origin, but completely re-done in the 18th century and only recently restored. The apse is the only part that remains of the original structure. The single-naved interior contains a bas-relief of the « **Madonna and Child** », in the style of Jacopo della Quercia, situated on the left of the entrance; near the right altar « **St. Anne and Madonna and Child** », a monochrome fresco uncovered during the last restoration works and attributed to Martino di Bartolomeo; near the main altar « **Coronation of the Virgin flanked by St. Peter and St. Paul** », triptych by Giovanni di Paolo dating 1445; fragments of other 14th century frescoes near the left altar.

Via dei Montanini then joins Via Garibaldi, where we find the **Church of St. Sebastian's Brotherhood,** in the Porcupine District.

Its construction was begun in the 15th century and two centuries later it was re-built; today it belongs to the St. Vincenzo de' Paoli Society. The interior display a rich 17th century decoration with paintings of the stories of St. Sebastian, by Pietro Sorri, Cristoforo Casolani, Rutilio Manetti and others.

Treasured near the altar is a wooden Crucifix belonging to St. Bernardine, who according to legend donated it to the Brotherhood of the Dead.

The Gonfalon Chapel contains a copy of the « Brotherhood's Gonfalon », painted by Sodoma in 1525; the original is kept in the Pitti Palace in Florence, where it was transferred in 1786; a Madonna, by Francesco Rustici can be found near the right chapel.

Going along Via Garibaldi, we also come to the Anglican Church of St. Peter on the right and then, on the left, an ancient house called **« La Consuma »** (meaning squander), because the story is, as recalled by Dante in Canto 29 of Inferno, that a lively band of pleasure-loving youths squandered away 200 thousand gold florins in twenty months (13th century).

Further on the road ends in the St. Lorenzo Barrier, situated in the North-western part of the city walls.

But now we shall go down Via Garibaldi and, on the right, we pass by VIA DI CAMOLLIA, where a little beyond the old Gothic building of the former Chigi-Saracini family, we find the **Church of St. Bartholomew,** of the Porcupine District. It was constructed in the 12th century and modified quite a number of times; the bell-tower is late-Gothic in style, while the interior is Baroque. The outer wall bears a fresco of the Redeemer. This church, which contains the tomb of Pinturicchio, preserves a **« Madonna and Child »,** by Vecchietta, **« Madonna and Angels »**, by the Sano di Pietro school, and a banner painted by Bernardino Fungai with the Saints Anastasio and Vincenzo, to whom the church is dedicated.

Along the same street, on the left, we find the **Arch of Fontegiusta,** from where the street of the same name begins, leading to the **Church of Fontegiusta.**

Built in 1482-84 to the designs of Francesco Fedeli and Giacomo di Giovanni, this church has a plain Renaissance facade in brick, with a marble cornice framing the portal, the work of Urbano da Cortona (1489);

The square-shaped interior is very interesting, divided by columns into three naves and covered over by decorated cross-vaults. The entrance wall: coloured stained-glass windows of the 15th century, made to the designs of Guidoccio Cozzarelli and depicting the **Madonna and Child between the Saints Catherine and Bernardine.**

Placed above the door are some weapons and the shoulder-blade bone of a whale, which **Christopher Columbus** was alleged to have donated to the Madonna of Fontegiusta. Legend has it that Columbus did in fact study in Siena.

Riccio's **« Visitation »** can be found in the arcade on the right of the entrance, while placed in the corner is a small 15th century bronze ciborium attributed to Giovanni delle Bombarde. In the arcade of the right nave we find a painting **« Jesus, Mary and Two Saints »,** which is probably the work of Francesco Vanni; on the right altar: **« Coronation of Mary and Four Saints »,** by Bernardino Fungai. Following this is an elegant choir dated 1510. Near the main altar we find a valuable marble tabernacle by Marrina, which frames a 14th century fresco. Marrina was helped by his assistant Michele Cioli, to whom the **Pietà** in the small lunette is attributed (1517); in the lunette above we find a fresco **« The Assumption »** by Girolamo di Benvenuto (1515).

Returning to Via di Camollia, we find the **Church of St. Peter at the Temple,** of the 11th century, though restored in 1942, which has an ashlar-work facade and a Gothic portal; a Renaissance brick chapel can been seen along the right side. The interior is of great interest for it comprises of a single nave, with a truss-work ceiling and a raised presbytery, and is adorned with 14th century frescoes. In the right chapel we have Riccio's fresco of the Madonna and Child.

Standing almost in front of the church is the house of the Sienese architect and painter, BALDASSARRE PERUZZI.

A little way ahead is the **Camollia Gate** that stands facing the road to Florence. This northernmost gate that dates from the 14th century,was re-built in 1604 to the design of Alessandro Casolani. The outer front of the arch bears these words of greeting to visitors **« Cor magis tibi Sena pandit »** (Siena opens her heart out to you much wider than this gate).

Continuing beyond the gate, we enter Viale Vittorio Emanuele, where we find the commemorative column of the

Porta Camollia

Antiporto di Camollia

meeting between Emperor Frederick III and Eleonor of Portugal on the 24th February, 1452 and propitiated by the then Bishop of Siena, Enea Silvio Piccolomini.

Following a short distance away is the grand « **Antiport** », comprising a high merloned portal almost completely of stone and dating from the 14th century. It was the most modern defensive barrier in the North of the city.

Straight after comes the **Oratory of St. Bernardine at Prato,** which treasures a beautiful Madonna and Saints, by Paolo di Giovanni Fei.

Instead, just one kilometre away, we find the **Devil's Palace,** later known as the **Turks Palace** and, today, the **Buonsignori Residence.**

Let's return to Via di Camollia and walk until we come to a cross-roads, where we turn down VIA DEI CAZZANI, on the right. Here we find the **Church of St. Stephen at the** « **Lizza** » (which means competition ring), re-built in 1641 over a preceding 13th century church. The interior contains: right altar: « **Visitation** » by Rutilio Manetti; main altar: « **Madonna and Child and Saints** », polyptych by Andrea Vanni (1400), with Giovanni di Paolo's predella bearing scenes of the **Crucifixion and Stories of St. Stephen;** left altar: « **St. Bartholomew** », a wooden statue by Guido del Tonghio.

The church overlooks the « **Lizza** », which is a beautiful public garden created in 1779 to the designs of Antonio Matteucci and, later, extended and embellished. At the opposite corner is the entrance to the **Fort of St. Barbara** or **Medici Fortress,** which is tied to the last heroic acts of the history of Siena, to those circumstances which accompanied the city's loss of independence, when in 1555, Siena was sieged by the Spaniards and the Medici

138

and had to submit as she was heavily outnumbered. Only two years later, Philip II of Spain gave Siena to Cosimo I who, in order to make himself more respected by the people, ordered the construction of the fortress, which is quite similar to the city walls of Lucca. In fact, the design was that of Baldassarre Lanci di Urbino (1560), who also took part in the construction of the other Tuscan city's walls.

On entering the fort, the first bastion on the left houses the **Italian Wine Cellar,** a permanent exhibition of all the different types of Italian wines.

Let's walk across the whole rampart, through the tree-lined avenues of the « Lizza », until we arrive at the rampart of the other side of the Fortress. We are at the border of the most ancient and better-preserved areas of Siena and the architecture here is typical of the 19th century middle-class architecture that can be found in any other city. However, just a few metres of road separates us from the heart of the Gothic and Renaissance architecture which can been seen in the city centre.

If we continue along the left side of the **« Lizza »,** beyond Piazza Gramsci, down Via Malavolti, we arrive in the lively and modern PIAZZA MATTEOTTI. In this square stands the Chamber of Commerce, the Post Office and Telecommunications Building, by Vittorio Mariani, and opposite, the **Church of St. Catherine** of the Dragon District.

From here we can go down VIA PIANIGIANI on the left or, better still, VIA DEI TERMINI, which takes us on a much more suggestive tour under very old arches and vaults and then brings us back to Independence Square. Going down Via delle Terme and crossing over Via di Città, we find ourselves once again in Piazza del Campo.

Fort of St. Barbara or Medici Fortress

THE PALIO

Even though the witnesses are scarce as to the origins and primitive features of the SIENA PALIO, one thing is certain, this feast which is the city's most popular and famous one, already existed before the year 1310, the year in which a document of Siena's General Council registers the official institution of the Palio: « To be run on the 16th August in honour of the Blessed Virgin ». And even if the mid-August Palio was originally only the high-light of a popular Feast Day, after the Battle of Montaperti in 1260, when the Sienese people conquered the Florentines, this event acquired even greater importance and in a political sense too. By the offering of candles the people wanted to render homage to the Madonna, to whom Siena had made a vow of subjection, as well as to reaffirm the Sienese commune's independence. Only in 1656, was a Second Palio officially recognized: the « District Palio » which is run on the 2nd July in honour of the Madonna of Provenzano.

The Sienese Districts, which came about almost by a natural process and out of the need for self-management in the light of a general break-down of the central power, were rather numerous in the 13th century and numbered about eighty in all. Gradually, these numbers were reduced to the present seventeen and certain changes were made so that today, these Districts do not only have a representative function, neither do they exist exclusively for organizing the Palio. In a certain sense they have reacquired their importance and significance: every Sienese is very loyal to his District, in fact, one can say that every individual lives in function with the Community which, in turn, repays him by following with interest and affection, all the most important steps in the individual's life. Life in the District bustles with fervour the whole year round, but in the days before and during the Palio, it explodes with excitement over the preparation and enjoyment of a suggestive and lively feast.

During the Palio, those who venture into the city streets, into those alleys that seem natural crevices in spite of being within the city walls, feel the air of a big feast. The drums on the eve of the Palio roll and break the time barrier, light the passions between one District and the next, let loose the old factious and heroic instincts of the Sienese people. It is the magical night of the impossible, the night of hope and prayer, of plots and secret agreement; of the pantagruellian meals and the ribald and provocative songs.

Finally, it is the day of the race. The characteristic flag of the District and Tertiaries flies at each corner of the main streets, at the wrought-iron rings on the buildings and, at the windows. In the morning, the Mass is celebrated in the Chapel of the Square, whilst the flags of the District and the Palio, destined to the winner, are brought for the blessing to the Church of St. Mary of Provenzano, on the 2nd July, and to the Cathedral on the 16th August. In the early hours of the afternoon, each horse, drawn three days prior to the race, is blessed in the District church. This « Barbarian », a half-breed so named because it

The « Propitiatory dinner »

once originated from Arabia, is the idol of the District and the protagonist of the race. The horse is watched over throughout by a stable-boy, called « Barbaresco » (meaning barbaric). Once the cerimony is over, the great procession begins to the incessant peals of the Mangia Tower bell, as well as to the fanfare of the high-pitched trumpets, the long silver trumpets of the Palio and to the deep rhythm of the drums.

This parade, so full of symbology that transcribes a thousand years of history, is definitely not superficial, but the actual essence of the Sienese people, the past, present and future, the hate, love and passion, the victory and defeat. Every Sienese, far and near, reads and writes his story in the Palio. Opening the procession are six mace-bearers of the Commune, followed by the flag-bearer with the page, carrying the white and black ensign of Siena. Next come twelve trumpeters with silver trumpets and eighteen palace musicians with their instruments. The Montalcino ensign goes past alone: this honour was conferred because of the loyalty shown to the ancient Republic. Then come the representatives of the five captains, the thirteen Estates and the eighteen vicarages, which at one time constituted the Sienese Republic. The procession continues with the flag-bearer of the Merchant Tribunal, followed

The benediction of the horses an riders

by the three Magistrates bearing the statues of Corporations, in parchment rolls. Next, eight standard-bearers of the Higher Arts Corporations, with 102 representatives of the people from the various Districts.

Now the Captain of the People makes his entrance, led by a page carrying the shield and sword. Then the three centurions of the City « Thirds », the three parts into which the population was divided, corrisponding to the three hills of Siena, and the three centurions of the « Masse », i.e. the inhabited areas, spread around the city walls. Next follow the representatives dressed in the costumes of the ten Districts which have been drawn to participate in the race, namely, a drummer, two flag-bearers, a captain, four pages, a standard-bearer and the rider mounted on the parade horse. Also the race-horse advances, which, together with the rider, is considered the District's idol. In the meanwhile, the two flag-bearers swirl their flags in all directions: each movement, carried out in perfect harmony by the artists, has a special name.

After a double row of pages carrying the symbolic laurel wreaths, it is the turn of the seven districts excluded from the race. Then follows the Captain of Justice, chief magistrate of the old Republic. Next, preceded by the Palace armigers, comes the huge cart bearing the « Palio », the much sought after piece of painted silk, and riding

on the cart are the four Biccherna leaders, eight Palace trumpeters, the page carrying the white and black gonfalon of Siena and a valet ringing a small bell, which was used to invite the soldiers to the altar before going to battle. The procession concludes with the parade of the suppressed districts; a suit of armour without a face and with the helmet visor shut. These are the six knights of the Cock, Lion, Bear, Oak, Strong Sword and Viper, whose suppression dates from 1675, following some incidents that occurred during the race.

Once the procession has finished, the horses mounted by their respective riders make their entrance from the Podestà Courtyard; each rider has a bullwhip, which is used to incite his own horse and hinder the other riders and horses. The participants line up in front of a thick rope of hemp and, when it falls to the ground signalling the start, the competitors dash off, urged on by the delirious crowd. This is a fast race – the horses complete three laps in just over a minute – and the most awaited and interesting part of the Palio; a tough and violent race run on a dangerous track with right-angled corners and steep slopes, and considered the worst track in the world by the riders, who have to ride without saddles and stirrups as dictated by the rules of this centuries-old ritual. And at the finishing line, a great roar of the winners fills the air accompanied by the roll of drums and the incessant pealing of the church bells. The winning District then lays on a feast and victory dinner, where the horse, with its hooves painted gold and wearing the caparison has a place of honour and eats sugar and fodder from a silver platter placed at the top of the Palio mast and which is inscribed with all the Palio winners' names. Really, the horse is the only true protagonist of the race: in fact, the

The « Mossa »

rules state that if the rider should fall off, both the rider-less horse and the District to which it belongs can qualify as winners.

All through the night the winning District and allies, carry the Palio trophy through the town streets to the rhythm of the drums and the swirling banners, shouting and jumping for joy. In Siena, the evening of the Palio is the time for joyous celebration and also the time for plotting vendettas and planning revenge.

Here is a list of the seventeen districts as well as the pages representing them, with the colours and coats-of-arms of each District.

The horse-race

TERZO DI CITTA'

This area comprises six Districts.

The Noble Eagle District (Aquila)

Its emblem is the two-headed eagle bearing the imperial crown and against the golden sun with the letters U.I. This emblem was conceded by King Umberto in 1887, the same year in which on the 16th July both Margherita and Umberto of Savoy attended the Palio. The District's flag is yellow with blue and black stripes and the headquarters are situated in Via del Casato di Sotto.

The Snail District (Chiocciola)

The coat-of-arms bears a crawling snail in the centre set against a silvery background strewn with roses and the initials U. and M. The flag is yellow and red with a blue border. Situated in Via San Marco is the 17th century church of Saint Peter and Saint Paul, which already belonged to the suppressed convent of the Nuns of Saint Paul. Since 1814 it is the Oratory of the Snail and its offices are located in the rooms adjoining the church.

The Flag-ship of the Wave District (Capitana dell'Onda)

This District's coat-of-arms has a dolphin with the royal crown floating in a blue sea. The Wave's colours which until 1714 were white and black, now are white and pale blue. The District headquarters are in Via Giovanni Dupré, near the picturesque arch of St. Joseph. Next door to these offices is the tiny church of St. Joseph which was erected in 1522 by the Guild of Carpenters and ceded in 1787 by the Archduke Pietro Leopoldo to the Wave District.

The Panther District (Pantera)

The insignia of this District is a rampant panther set against the letter U on a red and silver shield and the District colours are red and blue with white stripes. The tiny church of St. Quirinus and St. Juliette is in Via San Quirico and since 1957 it is the Oratory of the Panther District, which has its headquarters in the same street.

The Forest District (Selva)
The coat-of-arms displays a rhinoceros under a thickly foliaged oak backed by a golden sun in a blue field with the letter U. This District flies a green and orange flag with white stripes. Looking onto the pretty square of San Sebastiano are the District's headquarters and Oratory, which passed over to them in the year 1818.

The Tortoise District
The District's coat-of-arms is a tortoise in a golden field, with Savoy knots etwined with daisies. Yellow and blue are the colours of this District whose territory comprises the ancient nucleus of Siena. The Oratory was erected in 1684 by the same District residents and is dedicated to St. Anthony of Padova. Adjoining the church, in Via Tommaso Pendola, are the headquarters and museum of the Tortoise District .

149

TERZO DI SAN MARTINO

CIVETTA

This area comprises five Districts.

The Prior Owl District (Civetta)

The coat-of-arms has a crowned owl, perched on a branch against a black and red background with the letters U and M. Red and black are the distinguishing colours of the Owl flag. Its headquarters are in Via Cecco Angiolieri and the adjacent medieval court of Castellare degli Ugurgieri holds the Oratory that was constructed in the year 1935 by the District residents.

LEOCORNO

The Horned Lion District (Leocorno)

A rampant horned lion, or unicorn, stands in the centre of the coat-of-arms bordered in blue and bearing the motto « Humberti Regis Gratia ». The flag is white and orange with blue stripes. The headquarters are in Via di Pantaneto near the pretty square of San Giovanni Battista in Pantaneto and are commonly called San Giovannino. Recently the Oratory was transferred here.

The Noble Conch Shell District (Nicchio)

A silver conch shell on a blue background, topped by the archducal crown, two coral sprigs and a pendant formed by the Savoy knot entwined with two Cyprus roses all go to make up the coat-of-arms of this District. The flag is blue with yellow and red stripes. The headquarters are sited in Via Pispini and nearby the District residents e r e c t e d their Oratory in the year 1680.

The Vale of the Ram District (Valdimontone)

Commonly known as the Ram District for on its coat-of-arms there is a rampant ram with a crown and the letter U. The District's flag is red and yellow with white stripes. The headquarters and Oratory dedicated to St. Leonard belong to the Ram District since the year 1741 and are situated in Via di Valdimontone. R e c e n t restaoration work has returned to the pretty little church, constructed in 1173, its original romanesque aspect.

The Tower District (Torre)

The emblem of this District is an elephant bearing a tower on its back. The saddle-cloth which is red a white cross and the small flag with a silver cross were added after the year 1877. From the 16th century the flag has always been wine red in colour with white and pale blue arabesques. Via Salicotto is the centre of the District and in this street stands the beautiful headquarters and Oratory of St. James which belongs to the Tower District since the past four centuries.

TERZO DI CAMOLLIA

This area comprises six Districts.

The Noble Caterpillar District (Bruco)

A caterpillar creeping on a twig and wearing the archducal crown forms the emblem of this District and the coat-of-arms bears the Savoy cross. The flag is yellow and green with blue stripes. The Oratory, with the adjoining headquarters and museum, is situated in Via del Comune and was constructed in the year 1680 by the District residents and named after the « Holy Name of God ».

The Dragon District (Drago)

A winged dragon, with a crown and a small flag bearing the letter U forms the coat-of-arms of this District whose colours are red and green with yellow stripes. The church of St. Catherine acts as the District's Oratory and was assigned by archducal decree dating from 1787. The rooms adjoining the church function as the Dragon headquarters and they are located in Piazza Matteotti, which at one time was known as « Poggio Malavolti ».

The Imperial Giraffe District (Giraffa)

The coat-of-arms has a giraffe tied with a string held by a knoor. A ribbon at the top bears the motto « Humbertus I dedit ». The District colours are white and red. Since the year 1824, the Oratory is the lower oratory of the collegiate church of St. Mary of Provenzano, which keeps in custody the image of the Madonna of Provenzano and to which the local residents paid homage right from the late 16th century. The headquarters are in Via delle Vergini.

The Porcupine District (Porcospino)

Its emblem is a crowned porcupine on a silver background with red Cyprus roses and the Savoy knot. The flag is white with red, black and blue arabesques. Via Camollia is the centre of the District and in this same street lies the headquarters and Oratory dedicated to St. Bartholomew. The Oratory is an ancient church of the Saints Vincent and Anastasia and it belongs to the Porcupine District since the year 1788.

The She-Wolf District (Lupa)

The emblem is the she-wolf of Rome suckling the twins and the Sienese ensign. The white and red border has alternating red and white crosses. The flag is white and red with orange stripes. The headquarters and Oratory are situated in the 16th century church of St. Rocco in Via Vallerozzi, which already belonged to the St. Rocco Brotherhood and was then ceded to the She-Wolf District in 1786 by the Archduke.

The Noble Goose District (Oca)

A white goose with the royal crown and a blue ribbon from which hangs the Savoy cross make up the coat-of-arms of the District. The flag is white and green with red stripes. St. Catherine was born in the Fontebranda region and in her memory a Sanctuary was built on the same site where her actual house stood. The headquarters and Oratory are situated in the rooms adjoining the Sanctuary and they were constructed by the District in the year 1465.

THE SIENA SUBURBS AND PROVINCE

As an enjoyable complement to the tour of the city, we propose tourists some itineraries in the immediate surroundings of Siena and the province, which is one of the most impressive areas in Tuscany both for its artistic content as well as the wonderful landscapes and environments.

The suburbs give Siena a rather varied and harmonious framework: the countryside so bright with its many shades of green, intermingled with the cultivated fields and the woodlands, scattered with buildings and animated by the numerous roads. The gently sloping hillsides are dotted with small towns and villages, some of which go to form the Siena Fractions known collectively as the « MASSE ».

The farm buildings with their characteristic haystacks vary the landscape even further. The hill-tops are dominated by turreted castles or ancient convents with bell-towers. There are also a number of villas, some of which are considered jewels of architecture and art, and others have been transformed into luxury hotels, offering comfortable lodgings to their international clientèle.

ZONE 1
Basilica dell'Osservanza, Certosa di Pontignano, Castello delle 4 Torri, Montaperti, Castello di BELCARO, San Leonardo al Lago, Pieve di Ponte allo Spino and Sovicille.

BASILICA DELL'OSSERVANZA

Leaving the city from the Ovile Gate, we go down Via Simone Martini and then climb up Via Chiantigiana. At the crossroads leading to Certosa di Pontignano, we follow the high road always on the left, until we come to the Basilica dell'Osservanza, which is the most important monument in the immediate surroundings of Siena.

The church was erected in the period 1474-1490, to the designs of either Francesco di Giorgio Martini, or Giacomo Cozzarelli.

Some time ago, standing on this same site were a 12th century monastery donated to St. Bernardine and an early 15th century church, which was partially destroyed by air bombardment in January 1944 and faithfully reconstructed in brick, keeping to the original dimensions.

The church has a simple facade, preceded by a portico, and a high dome covered by a cylindrical cupola.

In accordance with their express wishes, Niccolò Piccolomini and Pandolfo Petrucci, two gentlemen of the city, were buried in this church, which is situated in an isolated and peaceful spot on the hill facing Siena.

The interior comprises a single nave flanked by eight chapels that are rich in art works, the most important o which are listed below.

Left Wall: 3rd chapel: **Madonna and Child between St. Girolamo and St. Bernardine »,** a triptych with predella by Sano di Pietro. **St. Bernardine's Reliquary,** by Francesco di Antonio (1454).

4th chapel: **« Madonna and Saints Ambrogio and Girolamo »,** a famous triptych once attributed to Sassetta, though today considered by one of the artist's followers known as the **« Maestro dell'Osservanza »** (1436).

The pillars of the triumphal arches bear some terra cottas by Andrea della Robbia, which depict the **« Annunciated Virgin and Archangel Gabriel ».**

Right Wall: 4th chapel: **« Saints John the Baptist, Francis, Peter and John the Evangelist »,** a polyptych by Andrea di Bartolo (1413). 3rd chapel: **« Crucifixion and Saints »,** by Riccio. 2nd chapel: **« Coronation of the Virgin »,** a terra cotta by Andrea della Robbia. 1st chapel: **« Madonna and Child and Angels »,** by Sano di Pietro.

The Sacristy, which contains a grand « Pietà » group by Giacomo Cozzarelli, has arranged nearby the AURELIO CASTELLI MUSEUM, which possesses a collection of paintings, sculptures, prints, seals and illuminated codices.

We leave the Sacristy and descend into the crypt and other halls that spread out underneath the entire church, which contain numerous tombs among which that of Francesco di Giorgio Martini.

St. Bernardine's cell has been constructed near the Loggia and it contains a terra cotta statue of the Saint as well as other relics and autographs.

CERTOSA DI PONTIGNANO

(Carthusian Monastery of Pontignano). This is situated at 8 kilometres' distance from the city, taking the route leading away from the Ovile Gate in the direction of Gaiole in Chianti and turning left just after the houses of Monteliscai.

Founded in 1343 and suppressed in 1810, today, this Carthusian monastery is the seat of the Mario Braccio University. It comprises three cloisters and a church.

We enter the first cloister, formed of high Renaissance arcades, and then via an elegant portal at the end we enter the second, smaller cloister of the 15th century and made of brick; then again, we pass into the third and largest cloister, which preserves the frescoes by Bernardino Poccetti.

CASTELLO DELLE QUATTRO TORRI

(Castle of the Four Towers). This time we leave the city via the Pispini Gate, taking the State highway to Arezzo, which stops at DUE PONTI, then we continue left along the road that crosses the railroad of Siena-Chiusi. The Siena landscape vanishes behind us and opening out in front is the wide Arbia Valley.

A little further ahead, a road on the right leads us to the Castle of the Four Towers, a severe quadrilateral construction, of the 14th and 15th centuries, which has a tower in each corner and a row of corbels. The castel's inner courtyard is very well-preserved and impressive.

Nearby, we find the Romanesque church of SAINT RE-GINA, founded in the 12th century and enlarged in the following centuries.
We then continue along the same road and, after some climbs up and down-hill, we come to

MONTAPERTI

A short path leads us to the Monteapertaccio hill, which served as the battlefield at the Battle of Montaperti. We can view the hillside, a monument, a few cypress trees, which mark the site where the castle once existed and which was the last desperate shelter of the Guelfs. Down there on the plain stood the Florentine cart stripped of its wheels and defenders while the Sienese ensign waved victoriously. Farinata degli Uberti, amidst the clamour of the Ghibelline victors, implored mercy for Florence. We are now entering the desolate « crete » zone, a sort of Tuscan desert, with its harsh earth that is tilled heavily today and only produces corn, no other fruit, neither any shady trees to shelter under in the summer heat.

Arbia as recalled by Dante: **« From the bare eroded calanques one then descends towards the poplars lining the banks of a tiny, pebbly river ».** However, straight after the river, we come across some scattered houses and more poplars; a number of cypresses every now and then and, stretching out in front, is a town with its houses arranged in steps and towers that reach up to the sky. We return to Siena and, outside St. Mark's Gate, we take the State highway to Grosseto. At the first crossroad, after Costafabbri, we turn right into a road that slowly crawls up between the hills, until we come to

Montaperti

CASTELLO DI BELCARO

(The Belcaro Castle). This construction dates from the 12th century and was later transformed into a Villa by Baldassarre Peruzzi, who built the residence, loggia and chapel together with Giuseppe Partini.

Also the frescoes adorning the various rooms are by the same Peruzzi. The castle is surrounded by a vast park dense with trees and cool shade.

LECCETO

About 5 kilometres from Belcaro, tucked away in a wood of holm-oaks, we find the Augustinian monastery which is very old and perhaps, dates from the 4th century.

It was suppressed in 1810 and, much later, was brought back to use as an Augustinian monastery, preserving its original aspect of a monastery-cum-fortress, surmounted by a beautiful tower of stone.

The monastery comprises a church as well, constructed in 1317 and extended in 1344, and later restored in the Baroque style. It has two cloisters, one formed of arcades supported by 13th century columns and, the other of the 15th century with brick pillars, remnants of frescoes on the walls and a well in the centre.

There is another 12th century Augustinian monastery not far away from Lecceto, however a large part of the construction has unfortunately been destroyed.

SAN LEONARDO AL LAGO

(St. Leonard at the Lake). The Romanesque-Gothic church,

San Leonardo al Lago

which was given its present aspect in the 14th century, preserves in the interior some remnants of 14th century frescoes by the Sienese school and follower of Pietro Lorenzetti. The apse contains some of Lippo Vanni's best works: groups of angels playing musical instruments, in the vault segments and other scenes depicting the life of the Virgin along the walls.

The Blessed Agostino Novello, Knight of King Manfred, was, at his death in 1309, temporarily buried in the crypt. Today, his remains are kept in the St. Augustine Church in Siena. From St. Mark's Gate we follow the State highway that leads via Roccastrada to Grosseto and, after about 10 kilometres, turn left in order to arrive at

PIEVE DI PONTE ALLO SPINO

(The Thorn Bridge Parish Church). It is an interesting Romanesque construction with a plain stone, ashlar-work facade, a notable apse and bell-tower decorated with single and mullioned windows.

The former monastery, which lies to the right of the church, is also interesting with the remnants of a cloister.

From this point we climb up towards the right and arrive at

SOVICILLE

Situated on the Eastern slopes of the Montagnola Senese region. The tiny castle, which was known as SUFFICILLUM in the Middle Ages, took an active part in the history of the Sienese Republic. It was sacked many times by the Pisans and Florentines until the year 1600, when it was almost entirely wiped out by a terrible epidemic.

Today it is famous for producing the valuable Sienese marble, which was already renowned in the 12th century.

ZONE 2
Monteriggioni, Badia a Isola, Colle di Val d'Elsa, Poggibonsi, San Gimignano.

For our second itinerary through the Siena province, we take the modern motorway uniting Siena with Florence, which takes us into the heart of Tuscany where we find that enchantingly beautiful town of VALDELSA.

Rich in an incredible variety of historical and artistic evidence, Valdelsa displays its extraordinary landscape wherein the vast hills appear blond with their covering of corn fields, the stepped stretches of vineyards, oak and acacia woods, alternating with silvery olive groves and, once again, the ever present cypresses that stand isolated against the sky. The houses are positioned perfectly, and dotted here and there are merloned castles with their suggestive, ancient low turrets.

About 14 kilometres away from Siena, the first locality that we come across is

« Monteriggioni with towers is crowned »

MONTERIGGIONI

a suggestive and glorious suburban town on the left bank of the Staggia torrent.

According to the wishes of the Sienese people, it was erected in the 12th century as a castle and served as the city's front emplacement against Florence. In 1213-19, it was encircled by a mighty wall, whose circumference was 570 metres and which had 14 huge towers that at one time stood much higher; they made an impression on Dante who refers to the towers in Canto 31 of Inferno: **« On the wall so round / Monteriggioni with towers is crowned ».**

The town still bears its medieval aspect and in the parish church we can clearly view the interesting example of the transition from the Romanesque to the Gothic style.

BADIA A ISOLA

(The Island Abbey). This little town, standing about 3 kilometres away from Monteriggioni, grew up around the Cistercian Abbey of San Salvatore, founded in 1001, which later became known as the « Island » on account of the marshland surrounding it.

Right up until the 14th century it assumed great importance, but from the 15th century onwards it saw a complete decline. Apart from the monastery buildings, the Lombard-type church was constructed during the 11th and 12th centuries and bears a facade crowned with small arches, wherein the remains of its original portal have been discovered. The interior, formed of three naves with an open truss-work ceiling, preserves some valuable works of art: on the right of the entrance is a rather damaged fresco by Taddeo Di Bartolo, and on the left, a Gothic-Renaissance style baptismal font in alabaster. The right nave contains a beautiful altar-piece, by Sano di Pietro, depicting the **« Madonna and Child and Saints »** (1471).

In the right apse we find an Etruscan-Roman urn bearing an inscription of 1198 and containing St. Cirino's ashes. Instead,

Panorama of Colle Alta

near the left nave we find a huge fresco, by Vincenzo Tamagni, of the « **Assumption, Apostles and Saints** ».
Inside the parish priest's house that is situated on the right of the courtyard, we find a beautiful and refined work depicting the « **Madonna and Child Enthroned** », which is attributed by some to one of Duccio di Buoninsegna's followers, while others consider it an early work by Duccio himself.
We now come to a detour on the motorway and turn down the State road No. 68. After about 2 kilometres, we come to

COLLE VAL D'ELSA

This densely populated and ancient town centre was first dominated by the Bishops, then formed part of a feud by the Aldobrandi family and, from 1333, it fell into the possession of the Florentines.
Right from the Middle Ages, Colle was famous and flourished thanks to her wool and paper industries. From the 15th century onwards, it became an important centre for the printing industry and the manufacture of glass bottles.
All these activities utilized the water energy source

supplied by the river Elsa and exploited by way of a channel system still in existence today. Like the other valley centres, Colle too appears divided into two suburbs, Upper Colle which has old medieval origins and was known as Castelvecchio; and Lower Colle, which has been enlarged by industries, shops, trading companies and residential areas. The ancient Upper Colle preserves 14th and 16th century walls and buildings, old gates and very suggestive medieval glimpses. We refer to the 16th century Campana Building and the daring arch that joins the St. Catherine Borough with the Castle; the Via del Castello area is rich in old houses, towers and residences of the 15th and 16th century; the Duomo, constructed in 1600 over a former Romanesque church, and the Pretorio Building dated 1355.

In Upper Colle, one can visit the ancient tower-house, the birthplace of Arnolfo di Cambio who was a famous painter and sculptor and who died in Florence in the year 1302. The huge square bordered by porches, is dedicated to him. This square forms the centre of the town life at Lower Colle of the Plain, and here we can find the beautiful Gothic church of St. Augustine, with its 13th century facade. The interior has undergone a Renaissance-type transformation carried out to the designs of Antonio da Sangallo.

Preserved here are a Madonna by Taddeo di Bartolo, a panel by Ridolfo del Ghirlandaio, a Deposition by Cigoli and a tabernacle attributed to Baccio da Montelupo.

Today, Lower Colle possesses a lovely, modern swimming pool, called « Olympia », and a beautiful park thus making it the haunt of many tourists and a sports centre for swimmers.

From Colle we go back onto the motorway which, in a few minutes, brings us to

POGGIBONSI

This is a modern and very active town situated about 25 kilometres from Siena, in the heart of Valdelsa. Un-

The Castle of Badia

doubtedly its geographical position, at the bottom of the valley and at the crossroads with major roads, has favoured the development of the trading and industrial activities of this centre. Its origins can be traced to the 13th century. With the destruction of the fort at **Podium Bonitii**, one of the strongest and most important Tuscan castles that was for a long time the bone of contention between the Sienese and the Florentines, the inhabitants gathered together in the castle of the Marturi village, where the old centre stands to this very day.

From the Mazzini Square, we climb up to the Church of San Lorenzo, which was erected in the 14th century, though largely re-built after the damage caused during the war, In the apse we can view a beautiful wooden Crucifix, dating from the first half of the 14th century and attributed to Giovanni d'Agostino.

Even the **Pretorio Residence** is of great interest, wherein we find some remains of the primitive Gothic construction, together with numerous coats-of-arms. Facing the building is the **Collegiate Church**, whose merloned bell-tower was once part of the old Marturi Castle. In the interior we can find a beautiful baptismal font in marble, dating from 1341, and a Resurrection attributed to Vincenzo Tamagni.

Some pleasant walks are suggested from Poggibonsi, such as that to **Castello di Badia, Castello Strozzavolpe** and the **Fairies Fountain,** with the beautiful ogival, Sienese-type arcades. From the Fairies Fountain, which dates from the 13th century, one can easily reach Rocca di Poggio Imperiale (Imperial Hill Fort), which was commissioned by Lorenzo the Magnificent in 1479 to Girolamo da Sangallo's project, unfortunately left unfinished; the Convent of San Lucchese tucked among the olive groves that comprises a church originally of the Camaldolesi and ceded to the Franciscan Order in 1213; and another convent constructed much later towards the year 1300.

Even though the church suffered serious damage during the war, it has managed to preserve a number of late-14th century frescoes, some by Bartolo di Fredi, a beautiful **altar-panel** by Robbia and an exquisite wardrobe with seventeen multi-lobel panels painted by Ugolino da Siena.

We shall now leave the Siena-Florence motorway and, after 11 kilometres along a picturesque road, we arrive in

SAN GIMIGNANO

This town is a very old centre of Etruscan origin, which in the 12th century became a free commune and whose history relates long wars with the neighbouring towns, most of all Volterra, and also fierce family feuds between the well-known Guelf Ardinghelli and the Ghibelline Salvucci families.

San Gimignano always sided with Florence and whose dominion it finally accepted in 1354. After this event, it went into decline and became the site of churches and convents, however, its development saw a recovery in the 16th century, when Cosimo I decided to build new

Piazza della Cisterna and the towers

walls around the town in place of the previous two, one erected in around the year 1000 and the other towards the end of the 12th century.

Although San Gimignano is located outside the reach of the big roads, it is nevertheless a modern and highly populated town, rich in artisan activities.

Still, its name and fame are tied most of all to its typically medieval aspect, to its innumerable art treasures and to the beauty of its surroundings. While nearing the town we can admire the wide landscape, stretching out on each side in an orderly coming and going of hills, farms, rural country houses and vegetation.

San Gimignano radiates her magical splendour all over this wonderful countryside. The splendid view of her towers is considered one of the most beautiful in the whole of Valdelsa, sweeping the distant horizon, beyond the valley confines, right up to the Pistoia mountains and the Apuan Alps.

The monumental centres of the town, which in its fabulous ancient aspect has preserved intact the roads, houses, walls, gates, famous towers – even if only fifteen still stand today out of the original seventy-two – are the **Cistern Square** with its two famous **Ardinghelli towers,** and the **Duomo Square,** which takes in the Collegiate church, the **Podestà Building** with its tall and mighty tower, and the glimpse of the two **Salvucci towers.**

The Cathedral or Collegiate: the interior.

The numerous and splendid paintings and sculptures are treasured in the main town churches and in the two museums. **The Civic Museum** is dedicated to painting and collects masterpieces of 13th century Florentine and Sienese painting, like the Cross by Coppo di Marcovaldo, or the Madonna attributed to Guido da Siena; 14th century art, for example the triptych by Taddeo di Bartolo; and 15th century art such as Pinturicchio's painting and the two wonderful « tondi » of the Annunciation, by Filippo Lippi.

The 13th century **Town Hall,** wherein lies the **Museum,** also boasts some famous frescoes such as Scenes of Family Life, by Memmo di Filippuccio and the grand Majesty by Lippo Memmi. The Diocesan Museum is, instead, dedicated to sculpture and the minor arts, such as embroidery, jewellery, illuminated manuscript, etc.

The **two** main sacred buildings are equally rich in art works. The **Collegiate,** erected in the 12th century and enlarged in 1460 by Giuliano da Maiano, is considered an exceptionally harmonious example of Tuscan Ronanesque architecture.

The interior is completely decorated with frescoes by Barna da Siena on the right, Bartolo di Fredi on the left, Benozzo Gozzoli and Taddeo di Bartolo on the entrance wall, which also bears two famous wooden statues of the Annunciation, sculptured by Jacopo della Quercia.

Finally, opening on the right is that jewel of Renaissance architecture, painting and sculpture, the **Chapel of Santa Fina,** which was created by Domenico Ghirlandaio and Benedetto da Maiano.

The other great church of San Gimignano is the Gothic building of **Saint Agostino or Augustine**, made of brick and dating from 1200. It is preceded by a suggestive little square and has an exquisitely styled Renaissance cloister. Inside the church we can admire the luminous altar-piece by Pietro del Pollaiolo, the frescoed ceiling depicting the stories of St. Augustine by Gozzoli, the altar-pieces by Pier Francesco Fiorentino, Giovanni Balducci and Vincenzo Tamagni, the most important local artist of the 16th century, as well as the chapel by Benedetto da Maiano.

Once out of the town of San Gimignano, we continue along the road leading to Poggibonsi and, if we return to Siena we may this time choose the Via Cassia.

The ever changing landscape will keep us enthralled: enchanting rows or plane-trees, alternated with wonderful views of the valley or its more intense sites, pretty villages and churches, rich in art works, endlessly follow one another.

We wish to point out **Staggia,** so famous and suggestive, with the conspicuous remnants of the town walls and their square-shaped towers, and the fortress with its sylindrical towers.

Its parish church dedicated to Mary of the Assumption, preserves apart from other things the early masterpiece of Antonio Pollaiolo entitled « Communion of St. Mary Magdalen », as well as a gracious Madonna of the 14th century. A little further on, on the right, we can view the **Lecchi Castle** set between the hillsides and corn fields

that gently climb up towards **Castellina**.
It is worth turning right to visit the ancient church of the
« Temple », dating from the 11th century.

ZONE 3
Buonconvento - Abbazia di Monte Oliveto Maggiore - Montalcino - Sant'Antimo - S. Quirico d'Orcia - Pienza - Montepulciano - Chianciano - Sarteano - Chiusi - Monte Amiata.

This third itinerary will take us on a tour of the medieval
parts of Siena's province, consisting of the area between
the Ombrone and the Orcia and bordered in the South, by
the Amiata as well as the mountains on which stand Radicofani and the San Salvatore Abbey.
In Siena, we take the Via Cassia which descends along
the Arbia valley and across the characteristic « Crete »
areas. After about 28 kilometres, we come to

BUONCONVENTO
which is also characterized, like may other centres in the
Siena province and in Siena too, by the encircling walls,
erected in 1300 over the ruins of the previous wall that
was destroyed by the Perugians. Buonconvento arose in
the 13th century on the same site of the once-existing
and ancient Percenna castle and it was an important defensive post for the Sienese Republic. On the 24th August,
1313, Emperor Arrigo VII died here. The parish church
houses an art gallery, where some interesting works are
displayed of the artists Sano di Pietro, Bartolo di Fredi,
Matteo di Giovanni and other less important ones.
About 9 kilometres away from Buonconvento, taking the
turning off the Via Cassia, the road climbs up to the

ABBEY OF MONTE OLIVETO MAGGIORE
situated on a solitary, wooded hill dominating the Crete
area.

This was the first abbey of the Benedictine Order of Monte Oliveto and certainly the largest and most beautiful among those that were erected in other localities and even in Tuscany.

Out of the midst of the dense olive groves and cypresses, the abbey emerges suddenly with the slender cusp of its bell-tower and, with the mighty and varied series of its projection that enliven the perimeter.

This complex, which is famous for its historical events and collection of masterpieces of art, comprises the monastery, cloisters, church, and the entire building as a whole, making it a sort of self-sufficient nucleus. It was founded in 1313 by Bernardo Tolomei (1272-1348), a member of Siena's most important family, who decided to abandon the world and withdrew to this solitary and unwelcome retreat, known as the Accona desert, which was his family's property. In 1319, the Bishop of Arezzo gave his approval to the institution of the Benedictine Order. In 1320, work started on the monastery's construction. Pope Clement VI confirmed the Monte Oliveto congregation in 1344. The abbey is still the normal residence of the general abbott of the Monte Oliveto Benedictine congregation.

This place, which is the favourite haunt of tourists, offers both a suggestive and pretty landscape, as well as an interesting art collection.

The church, which was erected in the 15th century and whose interior was re-built after 1772 in the Gothic style, possesses some marvellous inlaid choir stalls by Giovanni da Verona

The cloister: frescoes by Luca Signorelli and Sodoma

(1503-1505) and a lectern by Raffaello da Brescia (1518).
Also of interest are the frescoes by Luca Signorelli and Sodoma, done at the beginning of the 16th century and depicting
in 35 panels the life of San Benedetto da Norcia. This series
of frescoes runs along the four walls of the huge cloister, with
its suggestive atmosphere in a double row of Loggias, airy and
tall and with rows of characteristic pillars.
We wish to point out the refectory, with its 17th century frescoes
of three naves to the designs of Friar Giovanni da Verona
(1518). Here too, we can find some valuable art works.
From Buonconvento, one continues along the Via Cassia
until Torrenieri where a crossroads lies leading to

MONTALCINO

This locality was already inhabited in the Etruscan and
Roman times, and it is one of the most interesting minor
Tuscan towns. It was subject to struggles between Florence and Siena; after the Battle of Montaperti, it sub-
mitted to Siena. Montalcino was one of the military
strongholds of the Sienese Republic.
It is renowned most of all for its heroic resistance against
the troops of Clement VII in 1525, and the Emperor's
troops in 1555, and also for having been the last seat of

the « runaway » Sienese who, in 1555, tried to revive their free Republic, though without much success.

The Piazza del Popolo is the centre of the town and overlooking this is the **Loggia,** erected in the 15th-16th century, but later restored. Other interesting buildings are the **Town Hall,** the **Church of St. Egidio,** the **Religious Art Museum,** rich in beautiful works, pictures on panels and Sienese sculpture considered the most important in the whole region, and the **Fortress,** standing mighty atop of the hill, a shining example of military architecture that was erected by the Sienese in 1361. Leaving Montalcino from the Fortress area, we take the road that borders the Belvedere, offering a wonderful panorama of the Orcia valley and Mount Amiata.

After a few minutes we arrive in

SANT'ANTIMO

This town is famous for its abbey, which is considered one of the highest examples of monastic architecture and founded, according to legend, by Charles Magne at the end of the 8th century. It definitely existed in 812 and was a powerful Benedictine abbey, which entered in a struggle with Siena in the year 1202.

However, the end of the 13th century saw its decline. The church, which dates from the 12th century, has a very plain facade decorated with hanging bows forming blind arches. At the far end rises up the imposing square-shaped Lombard tower; the three-naved interior is characterized by the women's gallery running above the arches, creating a very suggestive whole.

The door on the right side leads down into the crypt, which perhaps dates from the 11th century. The remains of the Monastery can be seen at the side of the church, namely the Treaty Hall, which dates prior to the church's construction.

Once back on the State road, after about 5 kilometres, we come to

SAN QUIRICO D'ORCIA

It is an old suburb, situated in a pretty position on the heights and saddled between the Orcia and Asso valleys, and is surrounded by woods and olive groves, with the characteristic medieval houses, small bustling streets, beautiful buildings like the Chigi and Pretorio residences ancient gates such as Cappuccini Gate and Porta Nuova. San Quirico, which was once known as St. Quirico in Osenna, has a very interesting and beautiful **Collegiate Church,** dating from the 8th century and later reconstructed in the Romanesque style at the end of the 12th century.

The facade has a grand Romanesque portal dated about 1080, preceded by a vestibule on grouped columns. The right side too, has a Lombard-type portal, with mighty cariatids resting on Lions dating from the second half of the 13th century, and which some attribute to Giovanni Pisano, althought it is most probably the work of one of the artist's followers.

A third portal, dated 1298, and in the Gothic style, can be viewed in the right head of the cross-vault.

The Collegiate church's interior preserves a triptych near the main altar by Sano di Pietro, and a beautiful, wooden inlaid choir of the 16th century, the work of Antonio Barili.

From San Quirico d'Orcia, we leave the Via Cassia and take the State road No. 146 for Chianciano, a panoramic road leading to Pienza, Montepulciano and Chiusi.

After about 10 kilometres we arrive in

PIENZA

Placed on a hilltop, Pienza grew up on the site of the ancient Corsignano castle, the origins of which are unknown, according to the wishes of Enea Silvio Piccolomini, who was then Pope Pius II.

Being a true man of the Renaissance, and a perfect humanist, he wished to change this little suburb where he was born into a new town, moulding it into one unique and coherent Renaissance style.

Bernardo Gambarelli, known as ROSSELLINO, achieved this ambitious project, which is considered the first real example of urban planning in a town centre. He very quickly constructed or transformed innumerable other buildings of the town, during the period 1459-1462. The monumental centre of Pienza is the harmonious **Pius II Square,** overlooking which are the principal

buildings and where one can find the characteristic well designed by Rossellino. Rising up around this are the **Twon Hall,** the **Bishop's Palace** and the **Piccolomini Residence,** which is perhaps the most beautiful 15th century building, together with the Ducal Palace by Urbino.

At the end of the square stands the Cathedral, which was also erected to Rossellino's designs, over the site of the ancient Romanesque parish church of St. Mary. It is on the whole Gothic in style, though the facade is entirely Renaissance.

We also point out the 15th century Ammannati Residence, situated in Corso Rossellino, and the Gothic church of St. Francis, dating from the end of the 13th century.

A few kilometres of road, set in a hill panorama famous for its vineyards, and then surging upwards against the sky with its towers and buildings is

MONTEPULCIANO

which can be called Antonio da Sangallo's town, like Pienza is Rossellino's town. This is a very ancient centre once inhabited by the Etruscans, and even legend has it that it was founded in 715 by King Porsenna and named Mons Politianus. Montepulciano suffered long struggles

Piazza Grande: the Cathedral and the Town Hall

Palazzo Tarugi

that divided Arezzo, Florence and Siena and on account of all this fighting it only managed to enjoy longlasting peace in the 15th and 16th centuries.

The town map reproduces the shape of the elongated crest on which the town stood and, even today, it is bordered by the surrounding walls whose sturdy ramparts dominate the more recent constructions down below. In the higher area we find the fortress and monumental centre.
Numerous steep and narrow alleys under arches and vaults, together with the few remains of the Sienese Gothic architecture, are the town's few medieval aspects, because here the architecture is mainly the Florentine late-Renaissance style.
We mention below some of the more interesting buildings of Montepulciano.
Along the main street we find the Avignonesi and Tarugi Residences, the work of Vignola, the Cocconi and Cervini, by Antonio da Sangallo, the Market Loggias, perhaps by Vignola, and the Bellarmino Residence, the house of the future Cardinal Roberto.

We can also find here the Gothic-Renaissance church of **St. Augustine**, by Michelozzo, the church of Jesus and the church of St. Mary of the Servants, which dates from the 14th century but was re-built towards the year 1600.

Situated in **Piazza Grande,** the monumental centre of the town, are the Duomo, erected during the years 1592-1630 by Ippolito Scalza; the 14th century **Town Hall** whose facade is attributed by some to Michelozzi; the **Contucci Residence** by Antonio da Sangallo the Elder; and the **Tarugi Residence** by Vignola.

We also mention the Ricci and Neri Orselli Residence, which houses the **Civic Museum** and its interesting collection.
Isolated, at the foot of the hill on which stands the town of

Montepulciano, we find the **Church of St. Biagio** with its rectory made of gilded travertine that is considered one of Sangallo's masterpieces.

It is in the shape of a Greek cross and has a grey dome and bell-tower, solemn stone pillars and balustrades; the entire complex clearly demonstrates the artist's sheer genius.

Church of St. Biagic

We leave Montepulciano and then continue through the picturesque countryside until we come to

CHIANCIANO TERME

This was already well-known for its health spas at the time of the Etruscans and Romans and today, it is a pretty, lively and modern town.

The spacious parks and avenues, the hotels, boarding houses and leisure clubs, straightaway give one the impression of being in a thermal health spa. The Acqua Santa and Sant'Elena factories, founded to exploit the thermal springs that abound in this area, make Chianciano one of the best-equipped thermal health resorts.

It also possesses a very efficient and high level health care organization.

Lying just two kilometres away is an old village probably of Etruscan origin. Rising above it is a height and here one can find traces of medieval architecture in the **Sonti Manenti Castle,** the old **Podestà Building** and all along the beautiful panoramic route. Inside the **Church of the Misericordia,** we can admire a fresco by Luca Signorelli, while the Hall of Ancient Art (Religious Art Museum) houses a small collection of paintings by the Sienese and Florentine schools.

Establishment of the Acqua Santa: the Park

Establishment of the Acqua Santa and Sant'Elena

Panorama of Chianciano Hotel Quarter

Not far from Chianciano lies the town of

SARTEANO

This is a holiday resort, old in parts, which is situated on the slopes of Mount Cetona and dominated by a massive fort dating from the 15th century. It was inhabited right from Etruscan times, became a free Commune in 1280, then had to submit to Siena marking the start of its historical events. Preserved in the upper inhabited areas of Sarteano, which are criss-crossed by tortuous alleys and the encircling double wall, is the extremely suggestive atmosphere of the medieval feud that once existed. Apart from the notable buildings, we wish to point out the Church of St. Martin and the Collegiate Church of San Lorenzo.

Sarteano is also rich in **thermal springs,** which are known as « **Bagno Santo** » (holy bath). This mineral water that gushes out at a temperature of 24° centigrade, was well-known even in ancient times and today, it supplies two baths, around which one can find a modern and fully-equipped camp site as well as a pretty recreation park.

We take, once again, the State road to Chianciano, which curves between the hills on the Southwestern border of Valdichiana and leads us to

CHIUSI

Placed on a height and patched with fields and olive groves, Chiusi which is probably of Umbrian origin, used to be a very important Etruscan centre, especially during the 7th-5th century B.C. under the reign of King Porsenna.

Small urn with lid and roman statue sculpture

It joined the Roman Alliance and became an important military post. From the 4th century onwards it was subject to barbaric invasions and struggles between the major Tuscan towns and had to submit to various dominions until the 16th century, when it was incorporated in the Grand Duchy of Tuscany.

Chiusi's tourist attraction is tied to its rich archeological heritage and the very interesting. Etruscan tombs situated nearby.

Apart from the Duomo, erected in the 16th century and re-built in the 12th century, the Basilica with its grand interior, divided by 18 beautiful and different columns originating from ancient Roman buildings, and the bell-tower placed over the old Roman baths sculptured in tufa, the most important building is that of the **National Etruscan Museum.**

Here one can find sarcophagi, building-stones, where ancient dances and myths have been sculptured into the bas-reliefs of the solid, geometrically-squared bodies; the famous CHIUSINE CANOPIES, unique vases used for preserving the ashes after cremation, and extracted from the tombs that housed them 25 centuries ago; urns; statues dating from the archaic period (6th-5th century B.C.) and classical period (3rd and 2nd century B.C.); and, finally, Greek vases, amphoras of Attica, objects from the Roman period (2nd century B.C. - 2nd century A.D.). Also worth visiting are the town's immediate surroundings, where one can view the Etruscan tombs scattered here and there. Of these, the most important ones are the tombs of Pellegrina, Scimmia, and Grand Duke, situated near one another, and the tomb of Bonei Casuccini, known as the « Colle » tomb and dating from the 5th to the 3rd century B.C. These examples cleary display the type of architecture and the decorations of the Etruscan tombs.

We now leave behind Chiusi and the reign of the Etruscans with their precious tombs and hypogea, and abandon the soft and relaxing, hilly Tuscan landscape, heading towards the mountains, in between suburbs and forts all bearing some very suggestive names.

The road snakes, rises, descends and, finally, climbs up to the **RADICOFANI FORT,** an ancient castle under the dominion of Ghino di Tacco, who tried numerous times to conquer Siena but without success. All that remains of this impregnable fort, which was blown up in the 18th century by an officer of the garrison, are the mighty projections of basalt rock that form the foundation.

After **Radicofani**, we take the « Mountain » road linking the towns on the Mount Amiata slopes, which is a panoramic route offering some fantastic views of the rare beauty of this landscape.

Saddled between Val d'Orcia, Maremma, Umbria and Lazio, is the isolated and mighty trachytic cone of **Mount Amiata.** This extinct volcano forms the highest peak in South Tuscany. Gushing out from the once bubbling lava and now porous and trachytic rocks are the Flora springs, which are surrounded by woods dense with chestnut trees, beeches that for centuries cover the ancient crater's sides.

But now we shall take a tour around the mountain, through the towns that almost encircle the slopes like a belt. They are centres of ancient origin, so typical for the old nucleus of houses massed together along the narrow and steep roads. Here too, we can clearly see the medieval traces, an endless amount of castles that dominate from up above, or a famous abbey in the midst of a suburb that has grown up around it. Given their strong, high position bordering Tuscany, in the past these centres acquired a notable strategic importance and today, the remaining witnesses are the encircling walls and other fortifications.

However, the primitive nucleus is generally flanked by a modern part in those areas where the terrain offered favourable conditions for a modern building expansion.

The most important locality of Mount Amiata frequented as a holiday resort is the ABBADIA SAN SALVATORE, tucked away in a wood where one can find wild strawberries and raspberries and most of all mushrooms. It comprises entirely of the remains of this **Abbey** which was founded by the legendary Longobard King RACHIS, in the distant year of 743. Later it was reconstructed in the Romanesque style during the 11th and 12th centuries.

The single-naved interior possesses a beautiful wooden Crucifix of the second half of the 12th century and a crypt with 36 columns that are very interesting for their shapes and the variety of capitals and, which existed much before the church dating perhaps from the 8th century.

Lying a few kilometres away from the ABBADIA is PIAN CASTAGNAIO, a town dominated over by two towers up on the heights namely that of Aldobrandi and the Sienese one. In the lower area it is dominated over by the 17th century Bourbon del Monte Residence, which also overlooks the white clayey stretches down in the valley that is furrowed with the bright, sparkling light of Paglia.

Pian Castagnaio, the object of struggles between the Benedictines, Aldobrandi, Orvieto and Siena, is situated in the midst of beautiful woods of chestnuts, oaks, firs, ashes and Turkey oaks and is considered a very inviting summer and winter hill-station.

The Mount Amiata summit, lying at 1,738 metres, and on which stands a wrought-iron monumental Cross, can be reached from Pian Castagnaio, as well as from the Abbadia San Salvatore.

Monte Amiata - The Cross

Our town also takes in ARCIDOSSO, situated in the bordering province of Grosseto, which has managed to preserve along with the modern hotels and boarding-houses, also the old parts of the town, with the winding steep roads, houses of stone that have turned black and scratched, the ancient parish church and the fort. Further ahead lies **CASTEL DEL PIANO** which, like Arcidosso, waged an ancient feud with San Salvatore Abbey, another beautiful resort for holidaying in.

And then comes **SEGGIANO,** lying on a hillock with the 16th century Sanctuary of the Madonna of Charity, whose red cupola rises up above the olive groves, and **CAMPIGLIA D'ORCIA,** where two towers, one inside the town and the other outside, stretch up out of the spikes of rock, almost like sentinels guarding over the deep valley.

The last stop in our tour around Amiata is **SANTA FIORA,** again in the province of Grosseto, which is one of the most important centres in this area.

It comprises a modern part, developed in the last few years with the aim of exploiting tourism, and and old part which is ever so picturesque with the merloned towers, castle, the parish church of Santa Fiora and Lucilla that is Romanesque in style with Renaissance additions and which preserves a very rich terra cotta complex.

ZONE 4
Rosia · Abbazia di S. Galgano · Chiusdino · Monticiano.

Our fourth itinerary once again departs from Siena. We take the State road No. 73, Siena-Arezzo, that leads us to the Montepescali Hill at the border of the Maremma plains.

Once past Castalpino and Malignano, we come to the small suburban town of **ROSIA,** which is situated partly along the road and partly high up on the hillside.

The parish church of St. John the Baptist, dating from the 13th century, has a lovely Romanesque bell-tower opened by four floors of windows that are single at the bottom increasing to four-mullioned ones at the top. The interior contains a 14th century baptismal font in marble, which some attribute to Andrea Pisano and a Madonna, Child and Saints, near the main altar, set in an altar-piece by Guidoccio Cozzarelli.

About two kilometres away from Rosia, we find the **Vallombrosian Tower Abbey,** erected in the second half of the 13th century, with a beautiful square-based cloister bordered by three rows of Loggias.

But the most interesting art attraction in the Siena province is the

ABBEY OF SAN GALGANO
It was erected in the early 12th century by the Cistercian Order, on the same site where Cavaliere Galgano Guidotti of Chiusdini withdrew from public life to become a hermit

Abbey of St. Galgano

Church of Monte Siepi

and his church, which dates from 1224, is considered one of the earliest Gothic monuments in Italy. This grand abbey was erected around the church and soon became one of the richest and most powerful in Tuscany; the monks of the abbey were even called to administer the Duomo Trust and manage the Finance offices of the Siena Commune.

The decline began in the 15th century, later leading to the definite abandon of the convent and church. Today, all that remains are the boundary walls and the very high pillars with their elegantly sculptured capitals. The very suggestive air that surrounds this silent recess can be equalled to the beauty of the architectural structures inspired by the pure French Gothic style. Adjoining the church is the **Monastery**, whose only remains are the treaty hall formed of two naves supported by thick columns, the large refectory, the small monks' cells and a few remnants of the cloister.

The primitive Romanesque church of **Monte Siepi** rises up on the hill above and consists of a circular foundation at the centre of which one can view the rock where, according to legend, St. Galgano was said to have implanted his sword in order to worship the hilt in the form of a cross.

Next to the church, which preserves a Madonna by Niccolò di Segna, is a chapel containing a beautiful series of frescoes, by Ambrogio Lorenzetti, that are unfortunately rather damaged. From San Galgano one can also tour **CHIUSDINO,** where St. Galgano's birthplace can be found, or **MONTICIANO,** where a beautiful series of monochrome frescoes by Bartolo di Fredi, Giovanni di Paolo and Guidoccio Cozzarelli, can be seen in the treaty hall of the ex-convent of St. Augustine.

ZONE 5
Castellina in Chianti - Radda in Chianti - Gaiole in Chianti - Castello di Brolio.

At Siena we take the State road No. 2 and then, straight after No. 222, and begin our brief tour of Chianti, which is renowned for its wines and which stretches out between the Arno and Ombrone basins, situated between Florence and Siena. Its landscape is one of the prettiest in Tuscany, consisting of woods, undulating hills covered with olive groves and vineyards, and flourishing crops.

After Quercegrossa and the simple but harmonious Romanesque parish church of San Lorenzo, wherein lie some of the region's art masterpieces, we arrive in **CASTELLINA IN CHIANTI,** which dominates the Pesa dell'Elsa and the Arbia valleys. The fortress with its 14th century turret, that has been partly restored was once called Castellina dei Trebbiesi after the owners of the nearby **Trebbio Castle,** while stretching out below is the unrivalled and beautiful countryside.

From Castellina the winding road leads us to **RADDA IN CHIANTI,** which is a friedly suburban town that preserves its almost intact 16th century buildings. Also of interest is the Town Hall, which has a beautiful 15th century fresco, of the Florentine school, situated underneath the portal.

Continuing along the road that passes through the woods, we come to the Romanesque church of **San Paolo in Rosso,** one of the most remarkable constructions in the whole of Chianti, which is fortified and given a characteristic touch by the the huge cylinderical turrets that still exist around the apse.

Returning to Radda and once again taking the road to Siena, we straightaway turn left down a beautiful road passing through chestnut woods that offer vast sights of the Chianti mountains and Valdarno. Finally, we arrive at the **Montegrossi Tower** and the splendid **Coltibuono Abbey,** which dates perhaps from 1049 and whose most well-preserved part lies in the outer area of the mighty apse forming part of a long row of 17th century buildings that overlook the beautiful courtyard.

From Coltibuono one can easily visit **GAIOLE IN CHIANTI** that grew up on the same site where, right from early times – perhaps even the 17th century – the market place once stood, and around which a certain amount of houses sprang up.

Beyond Gaiole on the road to Montevarchi, one can find the **BROLIO CASTLE,** situated in a magnificent position on a hilly ridge. It has very old origins and the documents dated prior to the year 1000 generally refer to it as Broilio.

Since 1141, this castle is the property of the Ricasoli family. It was dominated by the Florentines, conquered many times by the Sienese and Aragonese and even partly set on fire. In 1860, Bettino Ricasoli ordered the complete restoration of the castle, though this was carried out in rather a liberal manner.

After the drawbridge, one may also visit the ramparts, which offer splendid views of the surrounding landscape: from Mount Amiata to the Arbia valley, right up to Siena and the mounts of Volterra. Also of interest are the ancient keep armed with towers, the family residence with its dining rooms adorned by valuable Flemish tapestries, and the armoury room containing period armour.

Situated in a small square is the **chapel of St. Jacob,** of 1348, which contains works by Segna di Buonaventura and other artists of the Sienese school. From here one can descend into the crypt that contains the Ricasoli family tombs.

In the valley below the castle, one can visit the buildings of the Ricasoli wine-cellar, which produces the famous and exquisite Brolio wines.

USEFUL INFORMATIONS

Numbers for urgent telephone calls:

EMERGENCIES	113
Red Cross (Misericordia)	280028
Hospital	46180
Police	41444
Carabinieri	212121
Traffic Police	47047
A.C.I. - Car assistance	116
Fire-Brigade	44444
Town Hall	280813
Municipal Police	280198
Telephone S.I.P. - Via Termini - 8-21	48490
Telephone from 1 a.m. to 6 a.m. - Via del Porrione	285296

OFFICIAL TOURIST OFFICE

Information and Publicity - Piazza del Campo 55	280551
Management & Administration - Banchi di Sotto 20	42209
Guide-Service: Informations at the ATA Travel Office	280551
Official « Viaggi SETI »	283004
Camping « Siena Colleverde » - Strada Scacciapensieri 37 - 1° April-15 Oct.	280044
Taxi (Telephone):	
Piazza Duomo	44107
Piazza Matetotti	289350
Piazza Rosselli	44504
Piazza Tolomei	42203

MUSEUMS-GALLERIES-CHURCHES (Opening Hours)

Palazzo Comunale (Town Hall) - Piazza del Campo
Public Rooms and Civic Museum, Mangia Tower: 1° October-31 March 8.30-13.30; April-30 September 9.30-19.30.

Picture Gallery - Palazzo Buonsignori - Via S. Pietro 29
Opening Hours: 8.45-13.45; Sundays 9-13. Closed on Mondays.

Cathedral Museum (Opera Metropolitana) - Piazza Duomo
November-February: 9-14; Sundays and other Holidays 9.30-13 - 15-18. March April May October: 9-13 - 15-18; Sundays 9-13 - 15-17; June July August September: 9-13 - 15-19; Sundays 9-13.

Piccolomini Library - Cathedral
Open from 9a.m. to the Cathedral closing team.

State Archives - Palazzo Piccolomini - Via Banchi di Sotto 52
Opening Hours: 9-13; Saturday 9-13. Closed on Sundays and holidays. Entrance free.

Archaeological (Etruscan) Museum - Via della Sapienza 3
Opening Hours: 9-14 on weekdays; on holidays 9-13. Closed on Tuesdays.

Municipal Library of the Intronati - Via della Sapienza 5
Weekdays: 9-20; Sunday and holidays closed. From 1° on 15 July closed. Entrance free.

Sanctuary and House of St. Catherine - Costa di S. Antonio
Open from 7 to 12 and from 15.30 to 18. Entrance free (Contribution expected).

Oratory of San Bernardino - Piazza S. Francesco
Apply to Custodian for visit to Museum.

SPECIAL EVENTS:

MAY 3-4: **National Celebrations in Honour of St. Catherine of Siena, Patron Saint of Italy.**

MAY 25 - Drawing lots at Town Hall for the three « Contrade » to take part, together with the seven entitled to compete, in the Palio of July 2.

JUNE 29 - In the morning, selection trials of the horses presented to the Municipality, and later « Consignment by lot » of the ten horses of the Contrade to compete in the Palio of July 2. At 19 o'clock, the Contrade will make the first trial run in Piazza del Campo.

JUNE 30 - The trial runs of the Contrade continue, in preparation for the Palio. They take place: at 9 in the morning and at 19 in the evening.

JULY 1 - At 9 a.m. the fourth trial run takes place, and in the evening the **dress rehearsal** is held. Late in the evening, the « propitiatory dinner » is held, attended by all the « Contradaioli », their agents and the jockey who will run in the Palio. Tourist wishing to follow closely these interesting popular manifestations, may also attend this dinner.

JULY 2 - THE PALIO

In the morning the « **provaccia** » (final test) takes place in the Piazza del Campo. Early in the afternoon, there is the benediction of the horses and riders who are to take part in the dangerous tournament. At 18 o'clock, the **Historical Procession**, greeted by the solemn notes of the bell from the Campanile of the Mangia Tower, enters the Piazza del Campo, and at 19 the race is run.

JULY 13 - Drawing lots at Town Hall for the three « Contrade » to take part, together with seven entitled to compete, in the Palio of August 16.

AUGUST 13 - In the morning, selection trials of the horses and subsequent « assignment by lot » to the « Contrade » taking part in the Palio of August 16. In the afternoon, first trial run in Piazza del Campo.

AUGUST 14 - The trial runs continue at 9 in the morning and 18.30 in the evening.

AUGUST 14 - Historical Procession of the « Votive Candle » offered to the Blessed Virgin of the Assumption, the Patron Saint of Siena and of its ancient State, in the presence of the Authorities and of the Pages of the 17 « Contrade ».

AUGUST 15 - Ceremonies in the Cathedral in honour of the Blessed Virgin of the Assumption, Patron Saint of Siena, in honour of whom the Palio will be run.

Official award of the gold « Mangia » and the silver Mangia », the symbolic decorations conferred upon those who have distinguished themselves for cultural, scientific and commercial activities for the benefit of the City of Siena.

The fourth trial takes place at 9 in the morning, and the « dress rehearsal » at 18.30.

Late in the evening the « propitiatory dinner » is held in the ten « Contrade » taking part in the Palio.

AUGUST 16 - PALIO

At 9 a.m. the **« provaccia »** (final test) takes place, and in the afternoon the benediction of horse and jockey who will run in the Palio. At 17.40 the Historical Procession makes its trimphal entry into the Piazza del Campo: symbolically, the glory of the ancient Republic of Siena comes to life again. At 18.30 the race is run.

DECEMBER 13 - Celebrations in honour of S. Lucia, with a market of ceramics, terracottas and majolica-ware which is held in the adjacent streets.

The dates of other events — or conferences of an artistic and cultural nature — are published in the Tourist Calendar Booklet, issued annually by the Official Tourist Office of Siena.

EXHIBITIONS AND MARKETS

Permanent Display of Italian Wines - Fortezza Medicea - Telephone 42.497.

This is the most important activity of the « Ente Autonomo for the Display and Sale of Characteristic and Vintage Wines. Opened in 1960, it was arranged with the assistance of the Ministries of Industry and Commerce, Agriculture and Forestry, and Tourism, as well as with that of the **Monte dei Paschi di Siena** and of the local **Chamber of Commerce.**

Housed in the 16th century Fortezza Medicea, the « Enoteca Italica » disposes of underground premises for the permanent display of Italian vintage wines which have previously been checked and selected by a special official Commission of Experts as a guarantee to consumers; there are also basement rooms for relaxation and wine-tasting in a suitably furnished, picturesque and welcoming setting.

A restaurant with menus suited for everyy one offers its services after the previous tasting.

HOTELS-PENSIONS-RESTAURANTS

HOTELS - Cat. Class Kat.

I   **La Certosa** - Via di Certosa 74 - tel. 288.180
I   **Park Hotel** - Via di Marciano 16 - tel. 44.803
I   **Villa Scacciapensieri** - Via di Scacciapensieri 24 - tel. 41.441
I   **Jolly Hotel Excelsior** - Piazza La Lizza - Tel. 288448
II   **Athena** - Via Mascagni 55 - tel. 286.313
II   **Castagneto Hotel** - Via dei Cappuccini 55 - tel. 45.103
II   **Continentale** - Via Banchi di Sopra 85 - tel. 41.451
II   **Garden** - Via Custoza 2 - tel. 47.056
II   **Minerva** - Via Garibaldi 72 - 284.474
II   **Moderno** - Via Baldassare Peruzzi 19 - tel. 288.453
II   **Vico Alto** - Via delle Regioni 26 - tel. 48.571
III   **Cannon d'Oro** - Via Montanini 28 - tel. 44.321
III   **Chiusarelli** - Via Curtatone 9 - tel. 280.562
III   **Italia** - Via Cavour 67 - tel. 41.177
III   **La Toscana** - Via C. Angiolieri 12 - tel. 46.097
III   **Lea** - Via XXIV Maggio 10 - tel. 283.207
III   **Senese** - Via Camollia 86 - tel. 48.324
III   **Villa Terraia** - Via Ascarello 13 - tel. 280.361
IV   **Bernini** - Via della Sapienza 15 - tel. 289.047
IV   **Centrale** - Via Calzoleria 24 - tel. 280.379
IV   **La Perla** - Via delle Terme 25 - tel. 47.144
IV   **Nuove Donzelle** - Via Donzelle 1-3 - tel. 288.088
IV   **Tre Donzelle** - Via Donzelle 5 - tel. 280.358
IV   **Tre Mori** - Piazza del Sale 19 - tel. 281.131
IV   **Pensione Palazzo Ravizza** - Pian dei Mantellini 34 - tel. 280.462

RESTAURANTS (giorno di chiusura)-fermée-geschlossen-closed)

Ai Tre Cristi - Via Provenzano 1-7 - tel. 280.608 (lunedì)
Alla Speranza - Piazza del Campo - tel. 280.190 (mercoledì)
Al Mangia - Piazza del Campo 42 - tel. 281.121 (lunedì)
Antiporto - Via Vitt. Emanuele II 79 - tel. 44.683 (sabato)
Castagnini - Via Massetana 68 - tel. 286.110 (martedì)
Chiusarelli - Viale Curtatone 9 - tel. 288.234 (sabato)
Da Ennio - Vicolo S. Pietro 4 - tel. 40.139 (giovedì)
Da Mugolone - Via dei Pellegrini 8 - tel. 283.235 (giovedì)
Due Pini - Strada di Malizia - tel. 46.003 (lunedì)
Girarrosto - Strada Grossetana 3 - tel. 394.006 (lunedì)
Grotta S. Caterina - Via Galluzza 26 - tel. 282.208 (lunedì)
Guido - Vicolo Pier Pettinaio 7 - tel. 280.042 (lunedì)
Il Biondo - Vicolo del Rustichetto 10 - tel. 280.739 (lunedì)
Il Campo - Piazza del Campo 50 - tel. 280.725 (martedì)
La Diana - Via delle Terme 5 - tel. 280.867 (martedì)
Le Campane di Beppino - Via delle Campane 4 - tel. 284.035
Le Tre Campane - Via Monna Agnese 5 - tel. 286.091 (venerdì)
Lo Stellino - Via Fiorentina 19 - tel. 50.259 (giovedì)
Medioevo - Via dei Rossi 40 - tel. 280.315 (giovedì)
Minerva - Via Garibaldi 72-74 - tel. 284.474 (lunedì)
Nello La Taverna - Via del Porrione 28 - tel. 289.043 (lunedì)
Renzo - Via delle Terme 14 - tel. 289.296 (giovedì)
Rustichetto - Via della Sapienza 41 - tel. 285.575 (lunedì)
S. Giovanni - Via dei Pellegrini 26 - tel. 288.079 (giovedì)
Self-Service - Via di Città 20 (sabato)
Serafino - Via Garibaldi 13 - tel. 289.251 (sabato)
Turiddo - Via Diacceto 1 - tel. 282.121 (sabato)
Vitti - Via Montanini 16 - tel. 289.291 (lunedì)
Zì Rosa - Piazza del Campo 13 - tel. 281.123 (giovedì)

Edito e stampato dalla

plurigraf

Narni · Terni

RO.MA.S.
L. 4.000